Redemption Song

The Boot Dance

Les Femmes Noires

Picture of Edgar White by Roy of Norland

This book is dedicated to
Montserrat (Alliouaga) – The Prickly Pear
The country of my birth

Edgar Monk White

By the same author

Plays

UNDERGROUND - 4 plays
The Wonderful Year (La Gente - The Workers)
The Burghers of Calais (The Scottsboro Boys)
Fun in Lethe
The Mummer's Play

CRUCIFICADO
Life and Times of J. Walter Smintheus

LAMENT FOR RASTAFARI (also includes)
Like Them That Dream (Children of Ogun)
Trinity (Man and Soul, The Case of Doctor Kola, That Generation)
(Published by Marion Boyars in one volume)

THE NINE NIGHT (also includes)
Ritual by Water
(Published by Methuen in one volume)

Children's Books

THE CHILDREN OF NIGHT
SATI, THE RASTAFARIAN
OMAR AT CHRISTMAS

This book has been published with financial assistance from the Arts Council of Great Britain

Redemption Song
The Boot Dance
Les Femmes Noires

Three Plays

Edgar White

Marion Boyars
London. New York

Published in Great Britain and the United States in 1985 by
MARION BOYARS Publishers Ltd
24 Lacy Road, London SW15 1NL and

MARION BOYARS Publishers Inc.
262 West 22nd Street, New York, New York 10011

Distributed in the United States by
The Scribner Book Companies Inc.

Distributed in Canada by
Collier Macmillan Canada Inc.

Distributed in Australia by Wild and Woolley,
16 Darghan Street, Glebe, New South Wales 2037

Distributed in New Zealand by Benton Ross Ltd
PO Box 33055, Takapuna, Auckland 9

© Edgar White 1985

All performing rights of these plays are strictly reserved and application for performances should be made to
Marion Boyars Publishers Ltd, 24 Lacy Road
London SW15 1NL, England

No performances of these plays may be given unless a license has been obtained prior to rehearsals

British Library Cataloguing in Publication Data

White, Edgar
  Redemption song; The boot dance; Les femmes
  noires: three plays.
I. Title   II. White, Edgar. Boot dance
III. White, Edgar. Femmes noires
822'.914

Library of Congress Cataloging in Publication Data

White, Edgar, 1947–
  Redemption song; The boot dance; Les femmes noires.
  I. Title: Redemption song. II. Title: Boot dance.
  III. Title: Femmes noires.
PS3573.H46A6   1985   812'.54   85-390

ISBN 0-7145-2837-4 Pbk

All Rights Reserved

Printed and bound in Great Britain by
Biddles Ltd, Guildford and King's Lynn

CONTENTS

Redemption Song   11

The Boot Dance   85

Les Femmes Noires   145

REDEMPTION SONG

The Son's Return

for Rufus Collins

First production – June 1984, Riverside Studios, London.
Directed by Charlie Hanson.

CAST

Mad Anne	Trish Cooke
Legion Bramble	Victor Romero Evans
Peter Bramble	Ram John Holder
Miss Beatrice	Carmen Munroe
Sores	Stephen Persaud
Mr Fowler	Malcolm Frederick
Verity Fowler	Janet Kay
Simon	Chris Tajah

CHARACTERS

Mad Anne	A villager
Legion Bramble	The returned son – a poet
Peter Bramble (Bad Bush)	The father – half paralyzed
Miss Beatrice	His aunt – owner of guest house
John Fowler	Merchant – a grave man
Verity Fowler	His young wife
Simon	The illegitimate son of Fowler
Sores	An albino, crippled

Location : The Caribbean. Any island to which a son returns in search of a father never known and a land half remembered.

ACT 1 – The Return

SCENE I – Invocation

Legion the son returns to the village of Redemption. Stage opens to blinding sunlight for re-entry to paradise. Sounds of Mento music: fife and drum. The street is filled with dancers as it is a mummers' festival at Christmas time (Jankanoo). Fowler is wearing a horse's head costume and is accompanied by the song:
   Horse head, come and gone
   Horse head, come and go way
This is the symbol that he is to be cuckolded. Legion kneels to the ground and kisses the earth. He asks several of the dancers for his father. Finally he approaches Mad Anne, who directs him to a man with a palsied leg and hand

MAD ANNE   Bad Bush, Bad Bush *(Man turns)* Somebody want you. This nice looking boy here. *(She laughs)*

LEGION   Are you Peter Bramble?

BRAMBLE   Who you is?

MAD ANNE   He too nice. Me could eat him right here. Come down for his Christmas.

LEGION *(Embarrassed)*   I'm your son.

MAD ANNE   Eh! Eh!

BRAMBLE   Which one?

LEGION   Legion.

BRAMBLE   Who you mother is?

LEGION   Pearl.

BRAMBLE   Oh God! You Pearl boy?

MAD ANNE   This you father for true? But how something sweet like you could come from Bad Bush?

BRAMBLE   Go way. *(Mad Anne kisses Legion and exits)*

BRAMBLE   Lord, make me see you. *(Inspects him)* But how you ain't write and let me know you - ?

LEGION   Mother said when you come to Redemption you must never let people know the day or the hour. Just come.

BRAMBLE   But where she? Pearl come with you?

LEGION   No, she never come. Just me.

BRAMBLE   But Lord Jesus, you is a man. Me son come look for his father. *(He sits down, wipes tears from his eyes and begins to rub his good leg with good hand)* Look everybody, me son come look for me, and I not even dead yet.

LEGION   *(Embarrassed)* Look, let me go get my things. I soon come.

BRAMBLE   Backside, if you would a let me know you was coming, I could of find some place for you.

LEGION   Oh, I figured I'd just stay at the house.

BRAMBLE   House? *(Pause)* Which house that?

LEGION   The house. *(Seeing the surprise on his face)* The house grandmother left me.

BRAMBLE   Oh, the house, you grandmother house.

LEGION   What's the matter?

BRAMBLE   Nothing, nothing. You go bring your things them. I take you to Miss B.

LEGION   Miss B?

BRAMBLE   Yeah, we sort out the other business tomorrow.

LEGION   Well, where you staying?

BRAMBLE   Me? Oh just here so so and there so so.

LEGION   Here so so and there so so?

BRAMBLE   I'll be all right now. You go bring you things them.

LEGION   All right. *(Starts to go)*

BRAMBLE   Legion... you mother, she still look... sweet? Boy, that hat nice.

LEGION   Yes father, she still look sweet. *(He gives father his hat, then exits)*

BRAMBLE   Lord, me son home. Me luck change. Me don't need no piece of old iron to keep the sea out now.

   Darkness

SCENE II

Outside of Miss B's guest house, 'The Viewpoint', which has seen better days

BRAMBLE   Now, you just remember to call she Aunt B.

LEGION   Is she my aunt?

BRAMBLE   Don't worry with that, anybody who have a bed give you at night is you aunt. Anyway, she me half-sister *(Pause)*. The wost half. Beatrice! Mistress B!

VOICE   Who that?

BRAMBLE   Is me, Peter.

MISS B   Bad Bush, what you want? I busy.

BRAMBLE   Is you nephew.

MISS B   Which nephew?

BRAMBLE   Legion. Pearl boy. Go kiss you aunt. *(Pushing Legion)*

LEGION   Hello, Aunt B.

MISS B   Well, my God, this Pearl boy for true?

BRAMBLE   He just reach from England. He's a big success and now he come search for he father.

MISS B   Which father *(Bramble gives her a look)* Well, come in, come in. You'll be wanting a room I suspect. We have quite a few tourist now, but I'll find you something.

BRAMBLE   Good, good. *(Makes to enter)*

MISS B   Is where you going?

BRAMBLE   I was just coming in for a –

MISS B   Not a rass.

BRAMBLE   Come on, Beatrice.

MISS B   This not Sunday. Me tell you could enter this house 'pon a Sunday. Other than that you keep you twist foot outside.

LEGION   Something the matter?

MISS B   You don't worry, son. Is between me and you father. He know what I talking. Right, Bad Bush?

BRAMBLE   Look B, the boy just come and I –

MISS B   Me don't have nothing to do with that. I'll see

to him. You just take your backside home.

LEGION   Look, dad, I could stay with you if you want.

MISS B   *(Laughs)* Him? Him no live nowhere.

BRAMBLE   It's all right, son. We talk tomorrow. Beatrice, you no easy. Sleep good. *(He exits)*

SCENE III

Legion seated on porch of house, eating breakfast. He looks out over the new land

LEGION   My first morning out of exile. The fields green and the hills green and waiting like a girl with new breast. *(Screams)* Redemption, I love you.

Enter Miss B

MISS B   All right?

LEGION   Yes thank you. Everything's beautiful.

MISS B   You sleep good? The dogs barking didn't keep you up?

LEGION   No. I slept like a dead man.

MISS B   That's good. Have to have the dogs because these people them tief too bad. So them a tief so them lie. *(Whispers)* And you better mind yourself, soon as them know that you here 'pon holiday they coming fe beg you drawers off you. You don't give them a damn thing. Country people wotless.

LEGION   Oh, I'm not on holiday, Auntie.

MISS B   You not?

LEGION   No, I come home to live.

MISS B   Live... here? You come Redemption fe live? *(She sits down)*

LEGION   Yes, I'm going to fix up my grandmother house and live off the land.

MISS B   Which land that?

LEGION   The land she left me. *(Miss B laughs)* What's the matter?

MISS B   You talk to you father about this land?

LEGION   We're going there today.

MISS B   Oh yes?

LEGION   Why you so hard on him, Auntie?

MISS B   Hard on him? Who, Bad Bush? Your father is the most miserablest bastard ever walk God earth. How somebody ain't take a cutlass to him backside is only Jesus know.

LEGION   You shouldn't talk like that, Auntie. He's just a sick old man now.

MISS B   What I have to do with that? Is his own fault. Is God lash him for all he wickedness. The man leap 'pon so much woman I don't know how his business don't rot off. His stones them big like coconut.

LEGION   Okay, Auntie.

MISS B   That man would a jump 'pon cow and all from him hear it have hole. Damn man a beast. *(Legion laughs)* But wait, what you mother tell you about him?

LEGION   She would never talk about him.

MISS B   Well, if she not talking, I not talking. Leave him to God. But you don't worry tell me nothing about my brother. Most I would do is feed him on a Sunday. One day a week, that's my penance. Other than that, me bury him when he dead so that people don't talk. *(Makes an instant turn and becomes the hostess again)* More tea?

LEGION   Thank you.

MISS B   *(Looking at sun)* Lord, it must be ten o'clock already. Boy no wake yet. Sores! Sores! Time you go town and get the ice.

A menacing albino figure on a cart emerges from beneath the steps of porch

LEGION   Flipping hell! *(Spills tea)*

MISS B   Say goodday to the gentleman, Sores.

Sores grunts

MISS B   He posing. Playing shy. Him mother run way and left him. Is me raise him. Them say albino is suppose to bring luck. Never bring me none. You go into town and bring the things from Fowler's.

LEGION   Is under there he stays?

MISS B   Well, I give him a room except now in the busy season. He don't need much space. There's not too much of him. He pays his way, though. Does odd jobs.

SORES   You want me clean you shoes? *(Turning cart suddenly towards Legion)*

LEGION   No, thank you.

MISS B   He do a good job.

LEGION   No, I clean my own shoes.

MISS B   You go town and bring up the things from Fowler's shop. *(Gives him money)* And mind they don't cheat you. *(To Legion)* Them have a coolie man work there now. He count too fast to suit me.

SORES   I hungry.

MISS B   Go quick and come back. You eat when you come. Have something nice for you. *(Sores exits)*

LEGION   How does he manage?

MISS B   Who, Sores? Don't worry, they strap it to the cart. His arms strong. So, you come back here for good? What you bring for me?

LEGION   Beg pardon?

MISS B   Beg pudding. Me ask you what you bring back for you old auntie.

LEGION   Well –

MISS B   Never mind. You having your car shipped over?

LEGION   Car?

MISS B   You is a big man. Go all high England and America. Don't tell me you don't have car. *(Looks up and sees figure approaching)* Wait. Bad Bush coming. You finish eat. I go put this food away. *(Grabs up remains of breakfast)*

BRAMBLE   Morning.

Miss B exits

LEGION   Morning.

BRAMBLE   Well, you sleep good?

LEGION   Yes, fine. I'm glad you came. We can go see the house now.

BRAMBLE   Boy, look like it go be well hot today.

LEGION   Yeah, pretty hot. We better get started.

BRAMBLE   Er... listen son, about this house –

Sound of laughter coming from inside. He looks towards door

LEGION   Yeah?

BRAMBLE   Come, make we talk. *(Leads him away)* You see, me never really know say you would a come.

LEGION   How you mean?

BRAMBLE   Well, you never write say directly that you mean for live *here*.

LEGION   I wrote you.

BRAMBLE   When? Last year you send little five pound at Christmas. I glad for it. Me take two drink and say well is me son send this *(Pause)* but me never know is here you mean to live.

LEGION   Look, Dad, what you trying to say?

BRAMBLE   Me no say nothing except... well right now, at this present time, the house kind of sell...

LEGION   How you mean, kind of sell?

BRAMBLE   Well, me never have the understanding that you would have ever come *(Pause)* directly.

LEGION   How you could sell the house? My grandmother left it to me. It was in my name.

BRAMBLE   *(Looking towards house)* Easy, easy. Don't let she see we quarrel. Come, we go the rum shop.

LEGION   I don't want to go rum shop. It's my house I want. The land.

BRAMBLE   Listen, you know how much a tax was 'pon

that land? I ain't make no big piece a money on the sale. You should be glad I take it off your hands.

LEGION   Glad? That's where I was born. I don't have fuck all else. When I was in England walking along the misery of Holloway Road. Waiting on some bus. Watching the dead walk. Old white people going home to eat dog food. West Indians with their hair gone grey from betting shops and rain. I say, 'Well, God, at least I know I have some place else.' This sentence not going be forever. The house I was born in, it come so real to me. *(Eyes luminous)*

BRAMBLE   Look, I sorry.

LEGION   Sorry?

BRAMBLE   What the rass you know about land? You a city boy. You can't deal with country.

LEGION   I could learn.

BRAMBLE   All my life me run a way from country. You feel it easy. All day long you walking in shit. Cow shit, goat shit, every kind of shit. In a city, a man could hide.

LEGION   This much I know: without land a man is nothing. Everything begins and ends with that. In England they stick you in any darkness and then charge you for being alive. For surviving.

BRAMBLE   Oh, so you feel it easy here because you have little piece of land. You see, these people, them like crab in a barrel. The minute them see you start to get somewhere, them want pull you back down. All them want do is tief it from you. Me tell you, you better off without it.

LEGION   It's not them I have to fear. Is my own father tief it from me.

BRAMBLE   *(Angelic face)* Son, how you could say such a thing? Suppose somebody would a hear you.

LEGION   I say it because it's fucking true.

BRAMBLE   What good the land was doing just sitting there? Taxes eating out me ass every year?

LEGION   You never pay them, so what you talking?

BRAMBLE   Still, it better it do somebody some good.

LEGION   But it was *mine*.

BRAMBLE   Well, is me you father?

LEGION   Father? What you give me? Ever?

BRAMBLE   Life.

LEGION   Yeah, and not fuck all else.

BRAMBLE   Well, after *that*, you suppose to make do. Is you owe me.

LEGION   Owe you... owe you? Yeah *(Searches ground and picks up a broken limb from tree)* here's what I fucking owe you.

Miss B comes from porch

MISS B   Legion! You can't do that. He wicked for true, but it bring you bad luck if you kill him. Come, what done is done. The house and land sell. Come, have some ginger beer.

LEGION   I'm going get it back, some way. *(Looks towards father)* I'm going get it back. To God. *(He follows Miss B into house)*

BRAMBLE   I feel for a cold drink, Bea. *(Miss B turns and*

looks at him. Sores enters on cart, package strapped to the side)

SORES (*After staring at Bramble for a good while*) Is you son that, Mr Bramble? (*Bramble shakes head*) Him big. (*Pause*) Seem like him want thump you.

BRAMBLE Why you don't mind you fucking business? You too damn fast. (*Makes to fling stone. Sores crawls away*)

Darkness

SCENE IV

Sunday afternoon. Enter the Fowlers. The Fowlers visit the guest house of Miss Beatrice. Mr Fowler is immense and sweating, with handkerchief always at the ready. His young wife, Verity, in a new dress and hat, can best be described as "country". His son, Simon, always seems awkward in his father's presence. They are about to enter the house

FOWLER (*Turns and looks in direction of parked car*) Simon, is there you mean fe left the car?

SIMON (*Turns and looks*) What's wrong?

FOWLER You can't see that it's in the sun? But what wrong with you, boy. You igronant or what? (*Simon looks bewildered*) Move the thing no, man.

Simon exits grumbling

VERITY Fowler, you shouldn't talk so to him, he's not a child, you know?

FOWLER Who say he's not a child? That one there is a loss, you hear me. Chupid as the day long, just like he mother. That's why me never marry her.

VERITY Shut you mouth. They go hear. *(Calls)* Miss B! Whoo ooo, Miss B, you home?

Miss B enters

MISS B Verity? You all right girl? *(Kisses her)* Mr Fowler, how you going?

FOWLER Suffering.

MISS B As much money as you make, and you suffering?

VERITY Don't worry with him.

MISS B That's a nice dress, girl.

VERITY You like it?

FOWLER Come my shop, could get you two on discount. Have a special shipment in from the States. Got my own man in Florida now.

MISS B That's all right. It look good on her but I don't think it would suit me. Come, sit down. I get you something to drink. *(Looks out)* Who that is?

FOWLER Oh that's just Simon mashing-up the car.

MISS B Mind the garden!

VERITY The place looking good. I miss it.

FOWLER You want come back and work here?

VERITY I wouldn't mind.

FOWLER You too lie. *(To Miss B)* Can't even get her to move these days, now that she lady of the house she sleep 'til noon.

VERITY That's not true.

FOWLER I just joking.

MISS B   Well, she have servant now. I don't blame her. Let me get you something. *(Exits inside)*

VERITY   Why you always saying those things? You know you won't let me do nothing in the house.

FOWLER   You not suppose to do nothing, that's what them have servant for. You not in bush'now, girl. You want shame me?

VERITY   No, but I don't see why if I go in the kitchen –

FOWLER   People will talk.

VERITY   But I get bored just sitting around, Fowler.

FOWLER   Ain't I buy you a video?

Simon enters

SIMON   Well, I park it.

FOWLER   *(Looking)* That's better. You must learn to to use you head. I'm not always go be around to bail you out and tell you what fe do, you know.

SIMON   *(Bitter smile)* Yes... I know.

Fowler looks at him. Miss B enters

MISS B   Well, here we are. *(Places tray with rum and glasses)* How you, Simon? How you like the police force?

SIMON   All right. *(Reaches for rum. Father looks reproachful. He surrenders bottle)*

FOWLER   He don't have nothing to do really. No big set of crime in Redemption. Most people do is tief food.

MISS B   These people too dam wotless. Even with watchdog you not safe. Them poison them.

FOWLER   Them just need a cut arse with a cat of nine tails. Them no tief again.

VERITY   People can't help it if they hungry.

FOWLER   If they hungry make they go wok.

MISS B   I'm with you there.

FOWLER   You see, the problem with these people is that nobody want work the land no more. Everybody want come town fe live and them can't do a Jesus thing but drop stick. I have no sympathy for them.

MISS B   Speaking of land... my nephew just come from abroad.

FOWLER   You nephew?

MISS B   Yes, Bramble boy.

FOWLER   *(Laughs)* Bad Bush?

MISS B   Yes, I think you know the property. It used to belong to Mistress Frances.

FOWLER   You mean that place by Cork Hill? Is me buy it.

MISS B   I know.

FOWLER   So what happen now?

MISS B   Let me call him. He could tell you better. Legion!

Miss B goes in

FOWLER   Well, if Bad Bush he father, I sorry for him. *(He laughs)*

MISS B   *(Returns with Legion)* Legion, this is Mr Fowler.

LEGION   Hi. *(They all stare at him)*

MISS B   And his son –

LEGION   Simon?

SIMON   Hey man, is you that? *(Grabs his hand)* I never know you come back.

LEGION   Yeah, I'm back, I'm back. *(Sees Verity and stares)*

MISS B   *(Noticing both the look Legion is giving and the expression on Fowler's face)* And this is Mr Fowler's wife Verity.

LEGION   *(Turns in surprise to Fowler)* Oh, very glad to meet you, Verity.

VERITY   A pleasure, I'm sure.

FOWLER   So you know each other, Simon?

SIMON   Sure man, we used to go school together. So what's happening? Heard you was in the States.

LEGION   Yeah, I'm back now.

SIMON   What you mean, for good?

FOWLER   What brings you back here? *(Sucking on ice)* Somebody chasing you?

VERITY   Fowler!

FOWLER   Just joke. But it's damn strange to come back to a little place like this. People retire here but you too young for that.

MISS B   He write a book. He's a poet.

SIMON   You lie.

FOWLER   Poet? What that is at all? You mean like Shakespeare?

MISS B   Look, I show you. I have it on the coffee table. Where everybody could see.

LEGION   Don't bother, Auntie.

MISS B   Let them see no. Soon come. *(She goes in)*

FOWLER   *(They all stare at Legion during the awkward pause)* So you is Bad Bush boy.

LEGION   I come to see about the land.

FOWLER   Which land that?

LEGION   The land my father sold you.

FOWLER   Oh yes, Beatrice mention something 'bout that. *(Lights cigar)* Well, can't really tell you nothing more than he sell it and me buy it.

LEGION   But it wasn't his to sell.

FOWLER   Well, me don't really know nothing 'bout that. All I know is him say was his so me buy um. Ownership is nine-tenths of the law. *(Pours drink)* Ain't that so, Simon?

SIMON   Nine or ten, I not sure which.

VERITY   You say the land did belong to you?

FOWLER   This man business we talking, Verity. Don't worry you head.

MISS B   *(Entering)* See it here. *(Holds book proudly)*

FOWLER   *(Taking book quickly before it reaches Verity's hand)* Well, let's see what we have here. 'Phoenix Rising'. *(Takes quick glance through book then takes mango from bowl and compares weight)* Not much weight.

LEGION   About as much as a life.

FOWLER   No man, a life weigh more than this. Me should know. I work as undertaker for ten years. *(He laughs, notices no one joins him)*

VERITY   Could I see the book please? *(Takes book)*

FOWLER   What's the matter? You people so funny. You like to pretend like you never go dead. You never want mention it. Well, is the one thing you can't hide from. The one business you don't have to go search work. It come to you. *(Pause)* You see, I tell this son of mine if he would a take up the trade he would be a rich man now.

SIMON   Not me, not a rass, me not in that. I don't want no undertaker trade. *(Pours drink)*

FOWLER   No, it's easier to be a rich man's *son*.

Simon stares at him

VERITY   The book seems very nice, Legion. Could I get a copy?

MISS B   Not this one. He sign this one for me. *(She hugs him and smiles)*

FOWLER   Well, since you is a big man with book and thing, you shouldn't have no trouble buying back the land.

LEGION   Buying it back? It had no right to be sold in the first place.

FOWLER   Is you father, ain't he?

LEGION   Yes.

FOWLER   Then him have right.

LEGION   What kind of money are you talking?

FOWLER   Around thirty thousand.

LEGION   Thirty thousand?

FOWLER   For the land – we ain't come to the house yet.

LEGION   I'll go to the law.

FOWLER   See the law sitting here. Me son police inspector.

LEGION   Simon?

SIMON   *(The silence of the world as he turns his eyes away)*

MISS B   Well, Simon?

SIMON   It could take a very long time.

FOWLER   *(Laughing)* You may as well appeal to God. Behold, the dreamer cometh. *(Sores enters)* Hey Sores, how you going boy?

SORES   All right, Maas Fowler sir.

FOWLER   Here, hold this for you Christmas *(To Verity)* Them say an albino suppose to bring you luck.

MISS B   Say "thank you" to the gentleman.

SORES   Thank you to the gentleman.

MISS B   Eh, eh. You too damn feistie.

FOWLER   *(Laughing)* Never mind. Well, time to go, we expecting company. *(Finishes drink)* Legion, you come see me when you ready, yes? You'll see me a reasonable man. Beatrice. *(Makes as if to kiss her)*

MISS B   All right, Fowler. *(Gives hand instead)* All the best, Verity.

VERITY   Miss B, I must stop and see you tomorrow. I have something fe ask you.

MISS B   Good, see you then. God spare life.

VERITY   Legion... Nice meeting you.

LEGION   Yes. See you again Mrs Fowler.

Verity looks at him

FOWLER   Verity, you coming?

SIMON   Look... We must talk, Legion. Get together, right? Be in touch.

They exit

MISS B   Me don't let that man kiss me. He smell a death.

SORES   He not an undertaker no more, Miss B.

MISS B   Me no care, he still a *grave* man.

Darkness

ACT 2 – AGON (Contest)

SCENE I – The Ritual of the Prickly Pear

Legion and Sores relax on porch playing Ludo

SORES   So what you learn over there?

LEGION   How to be invisible.

SORES   Invisible?

LEGION   How to wear dark clothes and move in shadows – that's what we do in England.

SORES   *(Wonderment)* That's all?

LEGION   *(To himself)* How not to make a noise when you cry.

SORES   *(Refusing to have his dream broken)* Well that's all right for you. At least you get a chance, you a been-to.

LEGION   A been-to?

SORES   Sure, been to England, been to America. Me just a wait.

LEGION   Not that great you know Sores.

SORES   When you go away you go write me?

LEGION   I'm not going.

SORES   Is so you say but you soon leave. Nothing no here. Just make sure you write me. I put it in my box.

LEGION   Your box?

SORES   *(Scurrying to his hiding place. Returns with old cigar box)* See it here. Is secret. Everything I love. I have some postcard, and see here some keys. *(Holds up keys proudly)*

LEGION   But what door they go to?

SORES   Me no know. *(Pause)* But me go find them.

Box falls over. A few coins fall out and a pair of lady's panties

LEGION   *(Picks up panties)* What's this?

SORES   *(Snatching them away from him)* She gave them to me. Remembrance.

LEGION   Who?

SORES   *(Pushing them in box)* She give them to me, I never tief it. You not go tell?

LEGION   *(Helping him pick up keys)* Why would I tell?

SORES   Is all right. *(Pause)* You have mother and father and thing. I don't know what that is. Me hold what there. *(Holds box)*

LEGION   Mother and father, cho, that's just trouble.

SORES   Why you say that?

LEGION   Because with parents first you expect and then you *owe*.

SORES   In this world, seem like them hard to keep. If them no run 'way leff you then is death tief them.

Enter Bramble singing

BRAMBLE   Hill and gully rider
Hill and gully
Hill and gully rider
Hill and gully

Bramble moves slowly across canvas, uncertain at first. He carries a sack and he smiles, full of teeth. Sings again

BRAMBLE *(Sings)*
    Emanuel Road man and boy
    here we break big stone man and boy.
(To Legion) How it going, son?

LEGION It goes.

BRAMBLE The postman and all ask me if me you father. You the poet father? Make me feel good. *(He laughs. Legion ignores him)*

SORES What you have in that crocus sack Mr Bramble? I see you wearing you burying suit.

BRAMBLE But tell me something, boy. Why it is you can't mind you damn business, eh?

SORES Is because me don't have much business, sir.

BRAMBLE *(Proudly)* Is something me bring for me son. *(Removes items ceremoniously)* See here.

LEGION What's this?

BRAMBLE Prickly pear. I notice that you hair dropping out. You rub you head with this and it soon grow. See how me care about you?

LEGION That's the first thing you ever give me.

BRAMBLE The second thing.

SORES Thing smell nasty when you put it on.

BRAMBLE Idiot! You don't leff in your hair, you wash it out.

SORES Oh.

BRAMBLE Anyway, son, I think you worry too much.

It never get you nowhere. You must learn to take it easy.

LEGION   Yeah, just relax and trust the world right. Everyone wishes me well *(Pause)* like you.

BRAMBLE   Yes... well... *(Reaches in sack again)* Look, I have a camera here. I want you take a picture. *(Hands him camera)*

LEGION   What for?

BRAMBLE   Send for your mother. Wait a minute. *(He fixes his clothes with his good hand)* Make sure you take it from me good side. Me don't want she see the hand.

LEGION   Dad –

BRAMBLE   Maybe I better sit down – no, I'll stand front the house. Always look better to have something big behind you.

He poses

LEGION   Dad, she doesn't want to know.

BRAMBLE   *(Kicking Sores)* Move out the way, boy. All right, ready.

LEGION   You don't understand.

BRAMBLE   Wait, let me plant my hat little bit. Hide up the grey.

LEGION   *(Flings down camera)* Goddammit, what do I have to do to reach you? She doesn't want to have anything to do with you. As far as she's concerned you're dead. You wasted her just like you wasted everything else in your life. Whatever you touch – Bad Bush.

BRAMBLE   What I do?

LEGION   What you do? Nothing, Dad. *(Pause)* You're good West Indian father. What you couldn't breed, you kill. What you couldn't kill, you sell.

BRAMBLE   You feel is me tief the land from you. You hate me for that. Land! What good is land when you belly-bawl and you arse hanging out. Land not for we. Land is for when God love you and you have money in a you hand and a woman in you bed. Land is for people like Fowler who don't need it. Me sell it rass yes, what else me could a do? You feel is me tief you? Well is not me, is life. *(Pause)* Life tief we. Don't make no sense to fight it. You may as well try feed meat and cake to the sea, like the Shango man them. But I swear, if me would ever know say that you would of come, me would have hold on to it. Even if me had was to suck salt because is one love I love. *(Pause)* But me can't talk that. Come, make me wash you hair. You coming old too fast.

He touches him with his good hand. They exit into the house, leaving Sores alone, who picks up camera from ground and watches them.

Slow darkness.

SCENE II

Verity comes to visit Miss B. They are folding sheets together in the yard. Miss B wears her sunhat proud and askew

MISS B   So is you one come, Verity?

VERITY   Yes.

MISS B   Oho. So what it is you want ask me?

VERITY   Well, I'm having trouble with the servants.

MISS B What trouble you having?

VERITY I don't really know how to talk to them. Some of them watch me so hard.

MISS B How you mean, watch you hard?

VERITY Well, I try and be friendly with them, I even give them some of me old clothes, but still is like they resent me.

MISS B Look girl, ain't no sense you worry to be nice with them. You must be hard, that's all them understand. When them see you not certain, is then them take liberty with you. Most you can do with a servant is to make certain them don't tief in the day, and don't breed in you house at night.

VERITY Maybe is because they see I'm so young.

MISS B Never mind with that. Young or not, you is the lady of the house. Is you must make them listen to you. Watch them good because you never know what kind of nastiness these servant girls does get up to. Some of them would even bring them manfriend quite into you bed the minute you back turn. Mark you, me know them.

VERITY You're right. I have to be more positive.

MISS B They just jealous after you. Don't 'fraid to take a stick to them if you have to. These girls not like you. When you used to work for me you was always decent. Carry yourself respectful and try and learn. These so, all them want study is *man*. *(Pause)* You know that I never tell you wrong, like when Fowler first come sniffing round you, me tell you was to wait and make he beg you for marry before he get what him want. And I was right, no true?

VERITY   Yes, Miss B. *(Pause and whispers)* He's a next one. You know he has his ways. Sometimes I don't really understand.

MISS B   What he do?

VERITY   Well... he won't ever let me get undressed before him. He never see me naked.

MISS B   Well, girl, some of these men funny so. A West Indian man don't respect no woman except he *mother*. Outside of she, all women is just to beat and breed. That's all them know fe do. So now, since him never see him mother naked, him don't want see you naked since you is he wife. Now, when he go outside to he night woman them is a different story. *(They laugh together)* They can't get naked quick enough. But you now must stay like he mumma. Pure. Anyway, is so he raise so what you could do, me dear? *(Secret touch on the girl's shoulder)* Anyhow, it sweeter to them when them can't see it plain.

VERITY   *(She smoothes her clothes with her hand)* Is over a year now we marry and nothing no happen.

MISS B   He not sleeping with you?

VERITY   Yes, but no pickny no reach.

MISS B   He use something?

VERITY   Him no use nothing.

MISS B   You using something? *(Thinks better of it)* No, of course not. Well, it must be God's will.

VERITY   Well, God will never too clear.

MISS B   By the way, you open your own account yet, like me tell you?

VERITY Well, no, him say he don't want me to have no bank book.

MISS B *(Laughing)* If I laugh I dead. So, if him tell you don't go toilet, you not going.

VERITY No, but anyhow me would open account him *must* hear. Is three bank in a town and him deal with all a them.

MISS B Well, me just hope you putting something away in case you dolly-house get mash-up. You could never tell with these men. Never mind he old.

VERITY *(Hearing someone)* Hush! Who that?

MISS B *(Looking)* Where? Oh, is just me nephew.

VERITY Well, I have to be getting back.

MISS B What's the matter, girl, is why you so frighten?

VERITY I not frighten, is just –

Legion enters

LEGION Hello.

VERITY Hello.

MISS B You go courthouse? You find out anything?

LEGION Everything shut down for the holiday.

MISS B Lawd, you walk all that way for nothing. You sit down. Fix you a nice cool drink.

Miss B exits leaving sly smile

VERITY *(After nervous pause, speaks loudly)* I'm sorry about your land.

LEGION I've been thinking on you.

VERITY   Oh, what you been thinking?

LEGION   Why you pretend not to remember me?

VERITY   *(Whispers)* You could see why. He has his ways. He wouldn't have like it.

LEGION   Seems like he used to getting it regular.

VERITY   Beg pardon?

LEGION   His way.

VERITY   Oh. *(Pause)* What's England like?

LEGION   A closet.

VERITY   A closet?

LEGION   Yeah, like living in a well kept closet. Neat. You see there's a shelf for everything. A shelf, a time, a bell. *(Imitates London chimes)*
  Ding Dong
  Ding Dong
  Dong Ding
  Ding Dong
For everybody. they move you about with a pair of pliers. They lift you up by your class.

VERITY   By your what?

LEGION   Class, love, class. And with a smile, the English smile. *(Demonstrates)* But if you're naughty and don't stay where they want you then they have a big, big dustbin called *madness* – where they mash you.

VERITY   Well, them have enough mad people right here. You don't have to go to England for that. But what about America? What that's like?

LEGION   If England is the closet then America's the

big plantation house. Same family, next generation.

VERITY   I wouldn't mind go there.

LEGION   You already there, love. You don't have to go to it. It comes *after* you.

VERITY   Legion, you all right? Is what them do you at all?

LEGION   I'm all right. I'm home now. Home. *(Staring into her body. She turns away)* Long time, girl, me never see you. *(Touches her)*

VERITY   What do you? You mad? Miss B coming.

Miss B enters, leaves drinks, eyes them and exits

LEGION   Listen, there's some papers I want you get for me.

VERITY   Which papers?

LEGION   The deed and the bill of sale. There's no record of ownership in town. Everybody is just giving me the runaround.

VERITY   So is that you want from me?

LEGION   No, but that will have to do for now.

VERITY   If he ever catch me is dead, I dead. You don't know that? Sorry, I can't help you. I gone. *(She gets up)*

LEGION   If I can't get it then I'll take something else. *(He tries to hold her)*

VERITY   You feel you bad.

LEGION   I'm bad yes.

VERITY   *(With mock scorn)* You could dead a bush.

LEGION   I'm dead already.

VERITY You Duppi then?

LEGION If you don't have land then you don't exist.

VERITY Look, you just leff me out of contention, yes. I know Fowler hard but is me husband. He's good to me. You gone away is how many years now? And now you want me for betray him. No, I'm sorry.

LEGION I don't want you to betray him, I just want you to help me.

VERITY No is the same thing? *(Steps away from him)* Tell Miss B I gone.

LEGION I'll walk you.

VERITY No, is all right. People them eyes too big.

LEGION Just a little way. *(Pause)* You glad you marry him?

VERITY Him help me. Him take me mother and them from bush. *(Pause)* We have two cars.

LEGION You could drive?

VERITY Well no – but we have driver.

LEGION Oh.

VERITY You laughing after me.

LEGION No. Girl, you pretty too bad.

VERITY Don't.

LEGION Remember when we used to drink sweet water in you mamma yard?

VERITY No... I can't remember.

LEGION I know a place. Remember where we used to meet?

VERITY *(Angry)* Me tell you me don't remember nothing.

LEGION Down by the graveyard.

VERITY Me 'fraid graveyard now.

LEGION Don't 'fraid graveyard girl. Is thereso we born.

VERITY Leave me no.

LEGION Listen girl, from time I love you like rice and you know it.

VERITY You too alias. *(He holds her)* Wait man, not here.

LEGION Where then?

VERITY Me can't –

Sores enters

SORES *(All eyes and smile)* Hello, Mistress Fowler.

VERITY *(Embarrassed)* Eh... hello, Sores.

She exits

LEGION Don't 'fraid graveyard girl.

Darkness

SCENE III

The porch of Fowler's house

FOWLER You all right girl?

VERITY Of course, why shouldn't I all right?

FOWLER What happen? Is like you want bite me. *(Pause)* You mother write you.

VERITY   Oh yes? Where the letter?

FOWLER   Inside. *(Verity starts to go in search of letter)* She say she need a next bed.

VERITY   *(Stops and turns)* You read me letter?

FOWLER   Wasn't nothing.

VERITY   What business you have with me mail?

FOWLER   But I always –

VERITY   Don't do it, right. Suppose I search up you things them?

FOWLER   What happen, you have something to hide?

VERITY   Look, you don't own me, you know, Fowler.

FOWLER   Don't own you? Don't own you? Is me dress you little claat remember. Is me feed you and you generation. Is me who take you backside from Mistress B yard and make you a woman.

VERITY   Why you never leave me there?

She runs off

FOWLER   *(Checks to see that the servants haven't overheard)* Listen Verity, me no mean nothing you know. The letter wasn't seal down Verity... Me not saying that you not good, you know. You save me lot of money. *(Pause)* You good for the house. Verity, I going town now. I bring you something nice when I come.

SCENE IV

Miss B's house, following day. Fowler enters angrily

FOWLER   Where the little bitch?

BRAMBLE   Who that?

FOWLER   Legion! *(No response)* Legion! Where you son?

BRAMBLE   You can't see nobody here?

FOWLER   I have business with him.

BRAMBLE   I see so.

FOWLER   Since that boy reach is problems. What he come for at all?

BRAMBLE   Well, is here he born.

FOWLER   He feel he smart. Well, me go show him me smarter.

BRAMBLE   What he do?

FOWLER   He come trouble my missus. Is fool. He feel me fool, but me have something for him. *(Takes out machete and sticks in wood of porch)*

BRAMBLE   Rass!

FOWLER   He feel me a poppyshow. I go do for him.

BRAMBLE   Wait, wait, come sit down man.

FOWLER   I don't want sit.

BRAMBLE   Why you feel say that my son interfering with you wife?

FOWLER   Since that rass boy come here she ain't have a good word for me. I catch she watching me from out the corner of she eye.

BRAMBLE   Well, that don't necessarily mean –

FOWLER   Wait. The maid say she can't see her in a the day time at all at all. Me want for know how she backside get so busy 'bout the place all of a sudden. She never used to go out. Most she would do choir practice. I say to meself eh eh, but this strange. Then this letter come to me office. *(Shows letter)*

BRAMBLE   *(Reads)* She horning you. *(He starts to laugh and then looks up into the grim face of Fowler)* Somebody just kidding you, man, don't take it serious.

FOWLER   You take this thing for joke. Well, it bloodclaat serious. How the boy could of do this to me? And me spirit did really take to him too.

BRAMBLE   Ain't you take the boy house and land?

FOWLER   What that have to do with it? One thing is business, next thing is life. Anyway, is you sell it.

BRAMBLE   But is you put pressure 'pon me with this tax business.

FOWLER   Everything me get me had to work for, you hear me? Hard. What me have me mean to keep. Why this rahtid boy no go back to rass England where he belong instead of trouble people them wife?

BRAMBLE   Is you wife you should see to instead of chase my son.

FOWLER   Well, hear me good, anyhow me find him near me woman me go chop him, right? And him blood must run, you understand? So me beg you tell him yes.

BRAMBLE   Man you age should be looking God instead of searching wife.

FOWLER   *(Walking off)* Just see you tell him.

BRAMBLE   Control you woman. You should put you foot up inna she cooker-hole. Hey, look you left you cutlass.

FOWLER   *(Turning)* Is all right, me have a next one.

Fowler exits

BRAMBLE   *(Taking up machete)* Backside!

Darkness

ACT 3 – Redemption

SCENE I

In town. Festival continues. Mummers on stage throughout scene. Bramble sees Legion and comes over to him

BRAMBLE   Legion. Come here no, mek we talk.

LEGION   Sir...

BRAMBLE   Somebody come look for you.

LEGION   Who that?

BRAMBLE   Who that? Fowler, that's who. Him say you trouble him wife.

LEGION   Don't worry with Fowler man.

BRAMBLE   Is not me for worry, is you. What you have with the girl?

LEGION   I don't have nothing with her. We just a talk.

BRAMBLE   Don't bother lie give me. *(Legion laughs)* Listen, boy, you know what a bullpistle is?

LEGION   No, sir. You tell me.

BRAMBLE   You take the dick from a bull.

LEGION   *(Laughing)* You kill it first.

BRAMBLE   Well, if you want try take it while it still alive you go on. You stop playing the ass and listen to me.

LEGION   Okay, sir. Sorry, go on.

BRAMBLE   You take the dick from a bull and you let it dry out. Now it could take all three weeks to season good. Now all the while a man know what he doing it for. He bite back him rage and swallow deep in him belly. You understand? Now, when the bullpistle ready, he come for you. Him hold it so. *(He demonstrates, miming the action)* Anyhow him catch you two good licks inna you rass with that you must fall. You laugh?

LEGION   I hear you.

BRAMBLE   You must learn to leave people them wife alone. Don't try for kill pussy because pussy will kill you. I know. I try and put up many a battle and you see *(Shows him palsied hand)* As you get weaker them get stronger. You must learn to leave some. You come meet pussy here and you leff it here. You think this here a joke? Fowler good to kill you, my son.

LEGION   Fowler just an old man.

BRAMBLE   Boy, when you have money you never old. What him can't do, him can buy.

LEGION   Well, there's one new thing he can't buy.

BRAMBLE   Mind how you go, me beg you. And watch out for his son.

LEGION   Who, Simon? I grow up with Simon man.

BRAMBLE   Ain't he is police?

LEGION   Yeah. So?

BRAMBLE   Nothing name *police* have friend. Them don't have mother, never mind friend. When you see policeman you just cross to next side of the road. You hear what me tell you. Don't even self walk the same side of the road. You cross over.

MUMMERS   The Riverbed come down
          The Riverbed come down
          The River come down
          And the graves they come open
          Way oh
          Way oh
          Way oh
          And how I can cross over?

Darkness as the two figures of father and son are frozen

SCENE II

Same as previous – in town. Legion is carrying the bag which his father had given him earlier. He approaches Sores who is seriously trying to catch a butterfly with his hands. The wheels of his cart make it impossible.

SORES   Rass! *(He falls over)* Is like trying catch God's shadow.

LEGION   Sores, I want you do me a favour.

SORES   What's that?

LEGION   I want take these breadfruit to Fowler's wife. Say that it's Miss B send them. If he's not watching, slip her this letter.

SORES   Boy, I don't know you know. I 'fraid that yard.

LEGION   Why?

SORES   Him have two murderous watchdogs. Them don't love black man.

LEGION   What kind of dog?

SORES   German Shepherd.

LEGION   That's not too bad. They could be worse.

SORES   Oh yeah?

LEGION   The one you want run from is the Rhodesian Ridgeback. Make German Shepherd look like a joke.

SORES   If they so easy why you don't go then?

LEGION   You know I can't.

SORES   Oh, yes. I hear that Fowler say he go do for you. Is why him hate you so?

LEGION   Because he tief me. Is guilt hold him.

SORES   Boy I glad me people did never leave me nothing. No house, no land for them to tief. The most them leave me is this cart.

LEGION   Mind that somebody don't tief that.

SORES   *(Sudden realization)* Is true. Lord, evil this world though, eh?

LEGION   Make sure you see her alone. *(Gives sack and letter)* If anybody ask you anything just say –

SORES   Is all right. Me could handle it.

As he moves off he encounters Simon, who stops the cart with his foot

SIMON   How you stay, Sores?

SORES   All right you know, sir.

SIMON   You there 'pon a mission?

SORES   Yes, Mistress B waiting.

SIMON   Oh well, you better go then.

Sores exits

LEGION   You all right, Simon?

SIMON   Just enjoying the holiday. How you never come see me?

LEGION   Figured you were busy about the Lord's work.

SIMON   No man, always have time for a friend.

LEGION   We used to have some good times. *(Pause)* Remember the picture shows? Eh. Cowboy and gangster... remember you were villain.

SIMON   No, wasn't me.

LEGION   Yeah man, we used to call you Villain.

SIMON   Was Freddie used to call so. Them call him Jack Palance because he so ugly.

LEGION   Yeah, Freddie, true was Freddie. Jack Palance. Well, who *you* was?

SIMON   *(Embarrassed)* Cisco Kid.

LEGION   Cisco— *(He laughs)* And afterwards was slingshot, stone and bottle fight.

SIMON   Bottle and stone to rass.

LEGION   And remember when Twist-foot loss his eye?

SIMON   Yeah, I remember. He should of run. *(Staring at him)*

LEGION   Twist-foot couldn't run.

SIMON   True. *(The silence of the world passes)* Remember you used to try sing like Sam Cooke?

LEGION *(Sings)*
>You send me
>You send me
>Honest you do

>   Honest you do
>   Honest you do
> *(They laugh)* What happened man?

SIMON   How you mean, what happened?

LEGION   To us.

SIMON   Nothing, just time.

LEGION   Good days, things made sense. We go down by the sea. It was always there.

SIMON   Is there still.

LEGION   Things different. Since I come back, I feel it.

SIMON   You must learn fe go easy, man. Stop trying to change things back. Accept until you could do better. You see these here? *(Shows his grin)*

LEGION   Teeth?

SIMON   These here so your *life preservers*. Them keep you afloat. If you want get through in this place that's what you have to do. Is best you learn it now. Don't try too hard because nothing is suppose to get done. You understand? So just drink you rum and eat you hog and rest yourself. Who in power stay in power. Father to son.

LEGION   And is your job to make *sure* that nothing gets done, right?

SIMON   What you come back for, Legion? What you really come back for?

LEGION   You know how many would come back if they saw a flicker of hope, just a match light even?

SIMON   Cho, they should be happy them could live somewhere else.

LEGION   Don't call it living really. The most you could say is marking time, keeping watch and waiting.

SIMON   If everybody who born here come back, the island soon sink.

LEGION   So then we're born for exile? You know, I feel them tief we youth from us.

SIMON   No must so?

> *Legion returns to circle of Mummers.*
> *They beat the ground in rhythm with their sticks*

SCENE III

Fowler's yard. Sores enters. He moves his cart, suspicious of the presence of the dogs. Verity has just come outside to smoke a cigarette in secret as her husband doesn't allow it

SORES   Mistress Fowler?

VERITY   Who that?

SORES   Sores, mam.

VERITY   Oh, is you.

SORES   I bring you something.

VOICE   Verity, who that?

VERITY   Is Sores.

VOICE   What him want?

SORES   *(Loudly)* Miss B send some breadfruit, sir. *(Whispers)* I bring a note for you. *(Gives note)*

VERITY   *(Loudly)* Tell Miss B thank you. These some nice breadfruit here.

Verity sits down on steps and reads note quickly
Sores stares at her and tries to look up her dress

VERITY   *(Catching him)* What you looking so hard for?

SORES   Something nice.

VERITY   You too damn fast.

Fowler enters

FOWLER   Why he never take it round to the kitchen?

SORES   She say I must give her personally.

VERITY   *(Taking breadfruits)* Thank her for me and tell her I go try come by there. *(Looks at Fowler)* If God spare life.

FOWLER   I smell cigarette. You smoking?

SORES   Is me, sir.

FOWLER   Them say it bad for you health.

SORES   So is poverty, sir.

FOWLER   *(Hands money to Verity)* Here, give him.

Fowler goes back inside

VERITY   Here. Tell him I can't promise but I'll try. Go quick.

SORES   Yes, mam.

VERITY   And thank you. I wish there was more I could give you.

SORES   Me too, mam. I would like somebody *(Pause)* I would like somebody in this world to know me.

VERITY   To know you, does it matter for what?

SORES   No, it no matter for what. Jus' so them know me. Somebody.

She kisses him. He exits

VERITY And when me say, mother me don't really feel to marry him you know, this man who make he money from grave, she say: Girl, when you black so like gully mouth what you could a do 'cept marry who you can and glad. Life not just finger ring and quick romance. You have a duty. You must look for you mother and family them. *(Pause)* Well mother, all right. You have fe say at least one of you children look after you. I give you two lives, yours and mine. But Lord, family could eat you flesh like beast.

FOWLER *(From offstage)* Vy, you staying out there all night?

VERITY Just now, Fowler.

Verity exits
Darkness

SCENE IV – Lament for death of Mockajumbie man

The mummers form a circle about Legion

LEGION The mockajumbie man dead, my friend
Mockajumbie man dead
He cut his throat 'pon telephone wire
Now police and soldier rule instead

Remember at Christmas how he'd come
With fife and drum and bell
Ten feet high on stilts he'd stand
Mockajumbie rise from hell

And him eye so red
And him face so dread
He scare us into truth

Well now mockajumbie man dead,
   my friend
And with him died we youth

Mockajumbie man dead, my friend
You no see mockajumbie dead
They cut him throat 'pon telephone wire
(Pause)
Now police and soldier rule instead.

CHORUS   Is dead he dead. *(In canon)*

Fowler enters the circle angrily

FOWLER   So what you is now, a prophet?

LEGION   No, a rememberer.

FOWLER   Yes well remember this, you rass, you. Me did warn you, right? Hand that stick give me! *(He grabs stick from one of the mummers)* Now me go batter you.

LEGION   I'm not go fight you. You an old man.

FOWLER   Oh yes, well dead then. *(He goes to strike him)*

LEGION   *(Sees Fowler is serious and takes up stick. The slow drum rhythm of stickfight ritual is heard)* All right, come then!

Fowler strikes at him several times until Legion sweeps him off his feet with a blow to his leg. Simon enters and stops the fight

FOWLER   *(To Simon)* Shoot him! Why you never shoot him? You too weak. You always was.

SIMON   *(Helping his father to his feet)* Come, go home. Come on, man, everybody watching you.

FOWLER   I don't care who watching me. You should shot him in a him bloodseed.

SIMON   How could I? What charge? What I could a shoot him for?

FOWLER   He too damn alias. He political. He just come here to mash up Redemption.

SIMON   Come, dad, mek we go home.

FOWLER   You too damn weak. You favour you mother.

SIMON   *(Suddenly lets go of him)* Is that why you never marry her? *(He walks away)*

FOWLER   *(Turns to Legion)* As for you, it no dead yet. You hear what me tell you. It no dead yet a rass.

> *Fowler exits*
> *Darkness*

SCENE V

Fowler's Yard. Simon brings Fowler home

VERITY   Lord, what happen?

SIMON   What I must do to please you, dad? *(Screams)* Tell me no?

FOWLER   Come a man.

VERITY   I ask you what happen?

FOWLER   Accident, me catch a fall. *(Pushing Simon away and walking with stick)* Never mind, me could walk.

> *Fowler exits*

VERITY   Simon, tell me the truth.

SIMON   You don't hear what he say? A fall. *(Pause)* Don't them say is women what cause man fe fall?

VERITY What you saying Simon? Speak plain no man.

SIMON Me not saying nothing. *(Turns to go)*

VERITY Simon, wait! Why you hate me so? What I ever do you?

SIMON Me say you do anything?

VERITY I feel it when you look at me.

SIMON You don't want me look, I won't look. *(Pause)* What I should call you anyway? Mother? Me feel a fool to call you so. How you like being Mistress Fowler? It sweet you?

VERITY So that's it.

SIMON It should a my mother be in that house, not you. What you know 'bout house? All you know is yard and bed.

VERITY Don't you ever talk so to me. Is not me take him 'way from you mother.

SIMON Is you yes. If is not you, then who? From the time him see you, you turn him fool and him can't see it.

VERITY Him would a never marry your mother regardless because he say she too too backward and wotless and – *(Catches herself)* Look, please don't make me cuss you here today right.

SIMON You mind how you talk 'bout me mother. You want me clap you?

VERITY You wouldn't venture.

SIMON *(Makes a step towards her and sees that she doesn't back away)* Cho! Go 'way.

VERITY   This is my house remember.

SIMON   *(Whispers)* He go soon done with you, you hear me. And I go be there, and then is go be me and you.

VERITY   I know is that you want, ever since. *(Quiet destruction)* Simon, tell me, you feel you could ever handle it?

SIMON   Me could handle it, to rass. *(Turns)* Me could handle it.

Simon exits
Darkness

SCENE VI

The graveyard. Verity enters; she is obviously frightened

LEGION   You come. I knew you would.

VERITY   *(Angry)* How you know? I just come to tell you please don't bother send no more message.

LEGION   That's all?

VERITY   Why you have to come back here? All you bring is trouble.

LEGION   Maybe to tief little love from out you heart.

VERITY   You could let go that. You just trying to get what you want. *(Pause)* Anyway, I can't find the papers you looking for so me no use to you.

LEGION   Is all right.

VERITY   *(Testing)* Is that you want right?

LEGION   Is you I want.

VERITY *(Turning away)* Me hear that when them interview you, you say Redemption is a place that eat its young.

LEGION Yes.

VERITY You can't say them things.

LEGION Why? Is true. Aren't they eating you?

VERITY *(Slowly)* Legion, people here live quiet. The first thing them go say is that you looking trouble. You want revolution.

LEGION You see this place, there's beauty, but we never see the fullness. Half the island is young but is old men in control. And who them can't control they drive away. *(Pause)* Like they did my mother.

VERITY *(Watching him like a stranger)* Is what them do you? Like you come back mad. Is just pure vengeance in you heart.

LEGION You see England, they never forgive a man for being a slave. You understand? I don't care how they invite you in and say history don't matter. They *never* let you forget. So I guess it matter, eh?

VERITY So what you could a do? You one alone.

LEGION Some man can just be glad to see they shadow 'pon a wall. *(Pause)* Me, I need more. I want come into a kingdom.

VERITY *(Laughing)* No kingdom coming again, man. Time for kingdom done.

LEGION So you never dream?

VERITY Dream... no. Nothing no come from dream.

Don't worry tell me 'bout dream. I'm all right, you know – have house and car and... Why you have to come? Why you have to come back now? I was all right... didn't feel nothing, didn't bother hope for more and now...

LEGION   Because I must know you again, to know myself.

He kisses her. Slow darkness of the graveyard covers them

SCENE VII – Revelations

Legion alone on verandah of guest house, finishing breakfast

LEGION   *(Working on poem)*
    You can tell the people I love
    You can tell them by the shoes they wear
    Shoes that travelled a thousand years along the edge of hope.

    You can tell the women I love
    You can tell them by their eyes
    Eyes that murder dreams
    Hands that cradle fire.

    Father, they tief my words but not my vision, not my vision.

Miss B enters, singing

MISS B   This is my story
    This is my song
    Praising my saviour
    All the day long.

After pause

    So, you is a stickfighter now?

LEGION   No, Auntie. *(Takes toast)* Wasn't my fault, you know.

MISS B   Tell me, how you getting on with Lawyer Stones and the house?

LEGION   Lawyer Stones, he want money. I don't have no more to give him. Money finish. *(He lifts cup for her to pour tea)*

MISS B   What! You mean to say you money done? *(She picks up teapot)*

LEGION   Yeah. *(Still holding empty cup)*

MISS B   *(Walking off with teapot)* Well, what you intend fe do?

LEGION   I don't know you know, but something must turn up.

MISS B   Oho! Something will turn up! Look boy, you staying up all night burning me electricity say you writing. You come in take two baths a day and you staying in there for must be a hour. Is me have to pay water rates, you know? If you want them length of time in a the water, you should go river and bathe.

LEGION   Sorry, I didn't know you had to pay –

MISS B   Oh, you must be feel government here a joke. The only thing free is rain water, you hear me? And a next thing, you just sit down there with your long foot them cock up and expect people to clean up after you. Look, everywhere is you rass papers. *(She picks up stack of manuscript papers)* Look here.

LEGION   Careful, they're all in – *(Scattered papers fall from porch)* – order. *(He goes chasing papers madly)*

MISS B Sorry, but you must be more tidy with you things. You don't have no servant here, you know. *(Watching the kneeling figure of Legion)* As a matter of fact, I think you better make you mind up to find someplace else. *(Legion suddenly stops and rises slowly)* I too old now to be supporting any man, you know.

LEGION I'm not asking you to support me.

MISS B Well, what you feel then, this is a free house?

LEGION No.

MISS B Mind you don't end up like you father, useless, and waste you life.

LEGION *(Returns to picking up rest of papers)* I don't really love the way you talk about my father, them kind of way there, is not good you know, auntie.

MISS B Eh eh. Oh yes? You father, you could tell him. Him know already how him stay: *useless*. Is God punish him for his damn wickedness. He drive you mother from out he bed, so he could bring in his nasty-ass woman them. You go ask him see if is lie me a tell. Father? You no even know you father. Ask you mother how much time she had was to get injection from them rotten woman disease he come bring her. Ask him why them call him Bad Bush. What happen you can't deal with it? Fire in you ass now? *(Begins to clean up: starts singing)*

> This is my story
> This is my song
> Praising my saviour
> All the day long.

(To Legion) Where you going?

LEGION I'm going get my clothes.

MISS B   You leff them stay until you have some money.

LEGION   Cho. *(Goes to walk in)*

MISS B   You want me to call police for you. Sores!

Sores approaches

SORES   Yes, Miss B?

LEGION   Never mind.

Sores sits

MISS B   And you don't worry come here unless you have some money bring me.

Legion exits

SORES   Me could have the room now Miss B?

Miss B stares at him

SCENE VIII

Location: fence by the sea. Legion and Bramble. Legion holding bottle of white rum between them. Time: Evening, the shadow hour when fathers fear their sons

BRAMBLE   So, you not going back?

LEGION   Never.

BRAMBLE   So where you mean to stay?

LEGION   In my Father's house is many mansions.

BRAMBLE   Which father that? Not this one, me could tell you. All I have is a piece of old iron over me. Not even room there to fart. You better go back.

LEGION   But what a way she hate you though, eh?

BRAMBLE   She don't hate – exactly.

LEGION   Yes, is hate. She hate you, *exactly*.

BRAMBLE   Well, me don't worry with her. Sometimes you have fe play fool to catch wise. You understand?

LEGION   But tell me, is what she say true? Did you really treat my mother all them kind of way?

BRAMBLE   Listen... you see this thing here, this same white rum which you drinking? Well, there's things which *it* do and there's things which *I* did do, but don't ask me which was which because me can't tell you. Right. When the rum hold you, you a next man again. I was searching the fullness. There was always something more of the world which I could never reach.

LEGION   You mean your soul cry out?

BRAMBLE   Soul? Where that is at all? When you hungry and you belly bawl is that you soul crying?

LEGION   No, but the soul cry too. That's part of you that remember God.

BRAMBLE   Remember God from when? Cho! Me don't know God too god. The Devil him I know. *(Pause)* I know the Englishman, the Yankee man and the Dutchman. From America to Surinam I know the Devil, and I see what him can do. God... well that's a different story. Him I never see.

LEGION   Everybody laughing after us, man. We the joke of the world. Coolie man and all laughing as they make money off us. Everybody have a country, a place. The Chinaman have China, the Indian India, the African Africa. What we have West India? We still just minding the plantation. Servant against servant, waiting.

BRAMBLE   Sometimes you must grin until you can do better.

LEGION   *(Screams)* Grin until when?

BRAMBLE   'Til you can do better.

LEGION   That's too long.

BRAMBLE   *(Touches Legion's hair)* Mek me see how you head stay. Your hair growing nice. Is the prickly pear that do it. You still there 'pon haste. You must learn go easy, son.

LEGION   Father, come let we go down. See the land, see the house, man. We have white rum. We could drive out the spirits.

BRAMBLE   What you talking boy? The land done sell. Tourist living there now.

LEGION   Is there I born. Nobody can take it. If I can't have it, then I burn it.

BRAMBLE   What you talking?

LEGION   What happened? They say when you were young you used to walk with rachet and gun in your waist. You never 'fraid anybody. What happen?

BRAMBLE   *(Eyes no longer luminous)* I catch a lash *(Pause)* So tell me about this poet business. How you really come to it?

LEGION   I started writing in prison.

BRAMBLE   Prison – what you doing in prison?

LEGION   Time.

BRAMBLE   For what?

LEGION   Stealing they called it.

BRAMBLE   But what the rass I'm hearing? So what you is, a poet or a tief?

LEGION   Sometimes it's the same thing, father.

BRAMBLE   So how you mother – ?

LEGION   Is she give me the money to come home.

BRAMBLE   But look 'pon me work here lord! So is why you come?

LEGION   I wanted you to teach me.

BRAMBLE   To teach you what?

LEGION   To build on the house. A next part. Maybe put up a windmill for power.

BRAMBLE   Windmill? The world done past that now, man. You a dreamer. You see this land, it look easy. Nobody that come here come for fun, you know. Anybody come here is for work, except for the old white people them. They come to fool death for a while. Even the trade wind is an undertaker.

LEGION   You know what I wish? I wish you never send me away, America, England. You never did me any favour, you know.

BRAMBLE   It was a chance.

LEGION   It was a sentence. *(He walks away)*

BRAMBLE   *(Singing)*
   Dark night ina the dungle
   When snake and mongoose meet
   Quashie bawl fe hungry

But Jan Crow bawl fe feast.
(Pause)
Walk good, son.

Darkness

SCENE IX - Three Lanterns

The sound of knocking at door is heard. Lights come up on the figure of Verity, who is covered with a shawl

VERITY   Miss B, it's me. Verity.

MISS B   Girl, what happen?

VERITY   Where's Legion?

MISS B   He not here. Must be with he father. We had some words. What you doing here this time of night?

VERITY   I leave him.

MISS B   You do what? Why you do something foolish so?

VERITY   Is like he gone mad. I tell him not to put his hand in me face. He tell me if I want go I could go, but I mustn't take nothing. He say I never have nothing when he meet me, and so I must go.

MISS B   But that man bad minded you know. Not to worry. You can stay here tonight.

VERITY   I feel he go do something you know, Miss B.

MISS B   Is because of the boy. Is through him that everything stir up.

VERITY   Is not his fault. All the while this was coming.

MISS B   Not his fault? You don't bother give up you

home for Legion. Him no have nothing fe give you. All him want do is wet you panty and breed you.

VERITY   Miss B, you never love nobody? You never want a man?

MISS B   Cho, done with that now, praise God. Old time people used to say, 'If you gnam pepper then you batti go burn.' I love one man but he dead leff me. Won't make that mistake again. *(Pause)* Come inside girl. *(She leads her in)*

Darkness

SCENE X – Crucifixion

Lights come up on Legion who has arrived at the property where he was born

LEGION   And there so was guava. And over here, mango trees. And mother Frances have her garden there and anything she eat she grow. And that road there would lead to teacher Biddie gate. Early morning to find me there or else is tamarand switch cross me legs and hands.

Facing teacher

But why I must learn my letters, teacher?
So that you can grow great and know the city.
Which city, teacher?
The city of God, and the truth will set you free.

He stands

Almost...
Well, teacher, is not quite so the world a go. Why you never tell me that you can have everything *except* where you were born?

>And so we come again to Redemption. Rum is my father, and my mother rice. *(He picks up discarded carnival mask)*
>
>*Three flashlights appear simultaneously; Rasta drumming is heard; the three encircle him, blinding him with their lights*

LEGION   Who there? Oh, so you come.

VOICES   Lick him—

>*The rhythm of the drums builds up to coincide with the ritual of stoning. There are three drums: the repeater drum echoes the striking of the stones, the deep 'funda' the heartbeat*

VOICE 2   He laughing?

VOICE 1   No, is dead he dead.

SCENE XI

Verity is beside the draped figure. Bramble and Sores in the background, frozen

VERITY   *(Sings)*
>Me say, me say reel and turn me
>Me say, me say reel and turn me
>You want me to go fall down
>Broke me belly 'pon tambourine.

>*Miss B enters and stands at grave site, dressed in black dress and white gloves, her eyes well acquainted with sadness. She hands money to Bad Bush from her purse*

MISS B   Say 'thank you'.

BAD BUSH   *(Painfully accepts)* Thank you... Bea

MISS B   Them say the sins of the father...

BAD BUSH   Still no love in you nowhere. You don't see the boy dead?

MISS B   I see too much funeral. Too much grave. I sorry.

BAD BUSH   What you have with me, Bea? Is what you really want, eh?

MISS B   What I have with you? Is mother give you all the love, what more you want? All she hope, all she praise was for she big *son*. And what happen when she take sick, wasn't me had to care her?

BAD BUSH   Well you was the girl.

MISS B   What girl? I was never a girl. Was me had to clean she backside. Me who had to hear she screams when night come. Sleep in her room, while you run off to chase you woman them. And still and all, the only one she calling for is you. You take me youth from me, Bramble. *(Pause)* Now look at you. And I'm glad you hear me. *(Softly)* Glad.

Bad Bush looks at her. She turns away and changes mood

MISS B   Anyhow, you son dead... You could come the house.

BAD BUSH   This not Sunday, Bea.

MISS B   *(Ignores his comment)* I fix you something... I know you like *(Pause)* cow heel. I could... *(She breaks off, looks toward grave and then runs off stage)*

Fowler enters with Simon. The sound of his stick is relentless and is heard before he is seen. Verity looks up, frightened

FOWLER You can come home now. *(No response)* Vy, you don't hear what me say? Me say you can come home.

VERITY No thank you.

FOWLER You better take the chance and be glad.

VERITY Be glad? What to glad about? All my life I do for other people. For me mother, for Mistress B, then for you. What to glad for?

FOWLER Listen , when you mother and the rest of you generation them eat bread and drink sugar water and call it dinner, was me who help you, remember?

VERITY You too lie. A who eat bread and sugar water for any dinner? Maybe me people them no have two and three cars, but them always eat good and share what them have more than a beast such as you would ever do.

FOWLER Yes, them give away too damn much, that's *why* them poor.

VERITY Me don't 'fraid you no more, you know. If you would a dead instead of he then I would have glad.

FOWLER *(Softly, almost to himself)* You don't think I know that? *(Turns to Bramble)* I... sorry them stone you son, sir. Here, take this help bury him. *(Hands him envelope)*

BRAMBLE But how you people could a wicked so? People don't stone people no more. Them is Roman times. *(Turns to Sores)* No true?

FOWLER Here, take the money, man. Is not me do it. Go on, take it.

BRAMBLE *(Spits in his face)* I dead first.

FOWLER *(Stops Simon who is about to grab Bramble)* No, is all right. Spit soon dry. Never mind with that. The two of we too old now for poppyshow. Nothing in this world free except death. You go soon have need a money.

BRAMBLE What police have fe say?

SIMON We'll... make... enquiries.

FOWLER You staying then, Verity? *(She doesn't answer)* Not to worry, is just a poet dead. *(With landowner's smile)* A next one soon come. Them grow like weed here. Must be the weather. Is best to stone them. Catch them at the root. *(Touches Simon)* You come a man now. *(Drops envelope at Bramble's feet, and exits)*

BRAMBLE Well, son, you ask what you have to do before they let you come home. Well, now you know. I did tell him, mind how you go. Speak the truth, yes, but mind how you a go because these people, them good to kill you. Too easy. Well, now you soul no bawl. Is that you come home for?

SORES Them say –

BRAMBLE What?

SORES Old time people used to say, 'Master God never shut a door unless him open a window.' Maybe... me could be you son, sir.

BRAMBLE Cho! You? You can't even walk.

SORES Well, that way me never will run leave you.

BRAMBLE Me have to write and tell he mother. Lord, *(Pause)* you could write, boy?

SORES   Yes sir.

BRAMBLE   Well come then. *(He looks at envelope on ground and is undecided)*

SORES   *(Seeing uncertainty)* Me will pick it up, sir. I closer to the earth. Have less way fe fall.

BRAMBLE   Sores...

SORES   Yes, sir?

BRAMBLE   Mind you don't run over me foot with that cart, I beg you.

SORES   Yes sir.

Bramble takes up his son's shoes, studies them carefully with the eyes of a scavenger, looks down at his own feet and decides to keep them

BRAMBLE   All right – come.

They exit, two figures moving across a dry earth, one moving more slowly than the other. The sound of Verity's song

VERITY   Reel and turn me
Me say, me say reel and turn me
You want me to go fall down
Broke me belly 'pon tambourine.

Darkness

Curtain

THE BOOT DANCE

First production – July 1984, Tricycle Theatre, London.
Directed by Alby James (Royal Shakespeare Theatre).
Designed by Sarah Jane McClelland.
Lighting by Dick Bloxidge.

CAST

Lazarus	Alton Kumalo
Gibbs	Jason Rose
Dr Adder	Lionel Taylor
Janette	Amanda Symonds

CHARACTERS

Lazarus Mphele   Black South African in exile
Gibbs   West Indian guard in asylum (early 40s)
Dr Adder   Psychiatrist (white, late 50s)
Janette Edwards   Patient in asylum (a half-caste), in late teens, fingernails well bitten by life

Author's Note

Setting	The circus of the theatre and the darkness of the asylum
Location	The city The entire play is viewed from the mind of Lazarus
Time	The human landscape of the present

ACT 1

SCENE 1 – Invocation

Music: *Tshona traditional South African, guitar and penny whistle*

Enter Lazarus Mphele. He is dressed in the traditional gumboots of the Boot Dancer. He enters to applause of audience which he regards with suspicion. He spreads sawdust as a spiritual and ritualistic protective device about the circle of the stage. He eyes audience then begins his dance. At that point where tension becomes maximal he experiences the entirety of his life, the leaving of South Africa, his ten-year exile in Britain. The dance ends. The applause of the audience gives way to the voices filled with echoes of family. A woman's voice most clearly is heard calling his name: Lazarus. He turns towards direction of voice. The pain of remembrance drives him to violence. He attacks audience with chair. He calls, 'Mamazina? Mamazina?'

VOICE 1   Kill the lights.

VOICE 2   Somebody hold him.

Darkness.
The voices continue to ring out in the blackness with the words 'Lazarus' and 'Mama' having an echoing feel. Briefly, under these voices we hear 'Mysterioso' by Thelonious Monk

SCENE II

Location: the asylum. Lazarus seated at table writing letter: he looks out to audience and speaks letter

LAZARUS   Dear Mamazina, I write to you because I do not want you to worry. You will not be getting any word from me for a while. I will not be able to send money just now as I am not myself. *(Repeats)* I am inside a large fish. The fish has eyes which watch me. It will be over soon, so they have told me *(Pause)* but they have lied before.

Enter Gibbs, the guard, singing, reading a copy of the Sporting Life newspaper

GIBBS   *(Doing an impression of Nat King Cole)*
There was a boy
A very strange enchanted boy
And though he travelled far, very far, over land and sea

Lazarus begins to tear up letter and tries to swallow it. Gibbs looks over top of newspaper at him

You all right boy? What happen? The food that bad in this place? *(Offers him newspaper to eat)* You want more? Is like you starving. Pressure reach? *(Lazarus merely stares at him and continues chewing)* Let me borrow your pen. *(He seats himself on table and begins to tick off entries of horses in paper)* Listen boy, nobody care who you writing, you know. You could write the bible if you want to. This not South Africa. Which horse you like? It got three here looking good: 'Kobo', 'Faustus' and 'Jungle Bunny'. *(Looks at him and laughs)* No offence. What you think? Could go either way, Piggott riding, but you can never tell with the 'Pig'. Yesterday I get wet and lose all me money 'pon him.

Lazarus has trouble swallowing – Gibbs slaps him hard on back

Should let you rass choke, you bitch you. I hear you wasn't a good boy last night. You kick up a whole heap of noise in the place. Won't let people sleep. I tell you, you must learn to keep you backside quiet when night come. *(Wagging finger)* This not Africa, you know. People don't bang 'pon drum when it get late here.

LAZARUS   I want... to see...

GIBBS   What? You talking today? Oh, me just knock your tongue back up out your throat.

LAZARUS   I want to see the doctor.

GIBBS   Who, Adder?

LAZARUS   Yes, Adder.

GIBBS   Well he's a busy man, you know.

LAZARUS   I want to see him.

GIBBS   You have to get an audience, just like the Pope.

LAZARUS   *(Screams)* It's my right.

GIBBS   Okay, man, okay. Rest yourself. I just kidding you. He's coming this afternoon. I go tell you something, though. If he find out about you keeping so much noise about the place, and eating paper and all, you go lose points.

Sound of laughter from another patient in hospital

LAZARUS   Lose points? What's that?

GIBBS   Everyone on a point system here, man. You build up enough points and you get to go out on visits.

LAZARUS   They let you out on visits?

GIBBS   Sure, if you're good. They let you out for a day.

LAZARUS   Where can you go?

GIBBS The park, a movie maybe. Might even let you go racetrack. That's a good place for mad people. They used to have a guy here name Striker. He always try to get a pass to go whore-house but them always catch him. He like to mash-up woman too much. And if you see him, he looks so quiet quiet and not much bigger than a dog. Striker. *(Smiles the good smile)* That man love pussy like Christ love a manger.

Laughs and then turns and sees that Lazarus is not joining in laughter

LAZARUS Who gives these points?

GIBBS The Owl.

LAZARUS The Owl?

GIBBS The doctor. That's what we call him.

LAZARUS Why?

GIBBS You'll see. *(Starts to walk off, then turns to Lazarus and smiles)* Tell me something. Why you mash-up that theatre like that? Is who you were trying to get?

Lazarus is silent

GIBBS Lazarus, me ask you why you try wreck the place?

LAZARUS You wouldn't understand.

GIBBS *(Confidential tone)* Was a woman, right? Is always woman somewhere in it, or else is God. Most of them that come here is one of the two. *(Pause)* But sometimes is voices. You look like a 'woman' problem to me. Is true?

LAZARUS   Tell me something, brotherman. Why are you a guard? You like your job?

GIBBS   A guard is a good job, for a West Indian. Anyway it suits me. *(Smiles)* Look, is not too bad here, this not maximum security. You could walk around *(Pause)* little bit. You behave yourself, you be all right. Hey, a dayroom there, you can watch little telly. Life sweet.

Gibbs exits

LAZARUS   *(Picks up his gumboots and looks at them. He then opens small battered briefcase which contains old photographs of when he first came to England)* Dear Mamazina. Have found lodgings in Notting Hill. One room, two windows, no sun between. I share the bath and sleep when the gas runs out in the meter. England will be all right, I think. If I lose my way, I never ask. I keep going until I find it. I try not to look a stranger. Mamazina, they let you walk anywhere here. Only... they have a funny habit, the English. When they see you're black, they cough. The rich cough into their hands. The poor cough in your face. But they all – cough.

Darkness

SCENE III

The office of Dr Adder. Several plants are visible. Dr Adder is present listening to some music on his cassette player, 'Blue Danube Waltz'. He takes a water tin and proceeds to water plants. He is a man in his late fifties, he wears the comfortable thick tweeds of old men and a pair of bright yellow cashmere socks. Gibbs, the guard enters. There is a wheelchair in corner of office

GIBBS   Lazarus is ready to talk to you now.

DR ADDER   Good, good, I didn't want to rush him. He's about due. How does he seem to you?

GIBBS   He won't trust me. He was writing a letter when I went in, he swallowed it.

DR ADDER   Bit extreme. All right, show him in.

GIBBS   Listen, doctor. *(Soft pause)* You think I could borrow a fiver until Friday? I have a sure thing on.

DR ADDER   Busy about the Lord's work again? Gibbs, do you know the difference between cash and credit?

GIBBS   No, you tell me, Doc.

DR ADDER   Cash is in the present, credit is always in the future tense. *(Takes out wallet)* Here's two.

GIBBS   Dammit! *(Taking money)* Should of ask for ten. Maybe I would of get five then.

DR ADDER   I doubt it. Send the patient in. *(Returns to watering plants)*

Lazarus enters. Stares first at the wheelchair and then at plants

DR ADDER   Come in, come in. It's hard to make anything grow here. Be right with you. Do you like Strauss? Sit down won't you. *(Looking at chart on desk)* Mphele, Lazarus Mphele. Well, how are you finding your little stay here?

LAZARUS   I... would like some medicine.

DR ADDER   What kind of medicine?

LAZARUS   A pain remover.

DR ADDER   *(Laughs)* Wouldn't we all?

LAZARUS   I need something to help me sleep.

DR ADDER   I see. Something to help you sleep. Yes, I think we could do something about that. Is this a recent problem?

LAZARUS   No, for a long while now.

DR ADDER   I see. Tell me, Lazarus – You don't mind if I call you that?

LAZARUS   It doesn't matter.

DR ADDER   Do you know why you're here?

LAZARUS   Because I'm not myself.

DR ADDER   Not yourself?

LAZARUS   The judge said...

DR ADDER   You've had a sort of breakdown. Do you know why?

LAZARUS   You're the doctor.

DR ADDER   But you're the one that did the breaking, which means you know more about the case than I ever could, wouldn't you agree?

LAZARUS   How do you know when you're crazy?

DR ADDER   You don't. You only know when you stop pretending.

LAZARUS   Pretending?

DR ADDER   Yes, everyone pretends to be normal, it's a game we play and we play it well most of the time. It's only when we stop playing that something goes wrong. Why did *you* stop playing, Lazarus?

LAZARUS   Start playing, stop playing. I don't know what you're talking about. I just want something for the pain, right?

DR ADDER How long have you been in Britain, Lazarus? *(Going to desk and taking out bottle of tablets)*

LAZARUS Ten years now.

DR ADDER From South Africa? *(Pours glass of water)*

LAZARUS Yes.

DR ADDER Why?

LAZARUS Why did I leave South Africa? *(laughs)* You must be joking. *(He sticks his hand out to receive tablet but the doctor swallows it himself)*

DR ADDER No, I could understand you wanting to leave South Africa, but why did you come to Britain?

LAZARUS I came with a musical. I was dancing. Boot Dance. *(Pause)* I thought that tablet was for me, Doctor.

DR ADDER What day was it?

LAZARUS *(Still staring at glass of water)* Was what?

DR ADDER The day you left South Africa. You remember it.

LAZARUS No, I can't remember.

DR ADDER Yes you can.

LAZARUS About the pain, Doctor

DR ADDER Pain? What do you know about pain? *(He turns off the cassette player)* Do you have any children?

LAZARUS No.

DR ADDER We have two children. A boy and a girl. A set. The girl is away, Switzerland. Her mother's country. Education's better there, expensive though. The boy's in school here. A fool. He should go far. *(He takes his own pulse)* They say that a son should speak with the enemies at the gate. I doubt if he could even find the gate, never mind speak. Stephan. *(Pause)* Tell me, don't you think that a father should be allowed to name his own son?

LAZARUS Well –

DR ADDER Stephan, that was her father's name. He made his money in chocolate but kept it in banks. Ever been to Switzerland?

LAZARUS No.

DR ADDER Good place to spend a war. You know what my only little pleasure is? *(Lazarus shakes his head)* I park my car and turn on my radio full-blast. Opera. The older you get the more you understand opera. *(Takes second pill. Lazarus stares in amazement)* Vitamins. I don't believe in drugging patients.

LAZARUS Listen, Doctor, I need some help, right?

DR ADDER Tea! Where there's tea there's hope. *(Starts electric kettle)* You know, Lazarus, life sometimes is not easy.

LAZARUS No shit, Doc.

DR ADDER Life's a bad job at best, yet we hold on, don't we? If youth could know and age could do. A young girl to warm the blood. *(Off in his own world)*

LAZARUS Pardon?

DR ADDER But we'll make do with tea instead. *(Takes out tea bags and cups)* Do you like opera? *(Hums.*

Lazarus stares at him)
La donna e mobile,
la la la la la.
No? Pity. *(Pause)* So tell me about the day you left South Africa. You remember it?

LAZARUS   Of course I remember! I remember everything. I hear every voice *so* clear, so clear. They get in the way sometimes, past into present. It was a Friday, the seventh of February. Mamazina at the airport. Her hat and her gloves. You would have thought she was going away she was so dressed up. I went to kiss her and some electricity... It must have been the carpet at the airport. I jumped away. She said it was a sign I would never see her again. I say 'No no, come on Mamazina... just a shock.' February the seventh, a Friday. The night before we drank all night at Babaleke's shebeen. All my friends... The mouths full of teeth and smiling. Everyone saying how pleased they are for me but... a bit of greed in the corners of their eyes. 'Yize Lazarus. He's a good one. Can dance his way out of Hell. Going up top, leaving Jo'burg, going with the angels. Dance Lazarus. The painted bird coming out of the sky for you.' I can hear my father's voice in my ears. He didn't come to the airport with us. He'd have nothing to do with it. He said goodbye to me outside the pondok.
'You'll be going among the dead now.'
'The dead, father?'
'White people are the souls of the dead come back. If you dance enough maybe they'll forgive you your blackness. Dance well, my son. Dance well.' Was it a blessing or a curse you put on me, father? Dance, Lazarus, dance for us. Dance, Lazarus.

Yize! *(He goes into the frenzy of the Boot Dance until exhausted)*

DR ADDER   Lazarus! *(No response)* Lazarus!

LAZARUS   But he never told me what happens when you stop dancing.

DR ADDER   *(Smilingly)* You know, Lazarus, others had the same problem.

LAZARUS   Which others?

DR ADDER   The Jews. Only instead of feet, it was hands. If you could play the piano or the violin well, you didn't have to go into the factory.

LAZARUS   You mean, they would forgive you?

DR ADDER   Yes, that was their Boot Dance. So you see you're not alone.

He starts to go and then turns back mischievously

Tell me, Lazarus, you remember the story of the little train who said 'I can'?

LAZARUS   The little train?

DR ADDER   Yes. No matter how difficult and twisting the path, the little train would huff and puff, 'Yes I can, yes I can, yes I can' all the way up the hill. His faith carried him on. *(He bends low and makes the sound of a train engine)*

LAZARUS   *(Looking at him)* You all right, Doc?

DR ADDER   Remember that little train, Lazarus.

LAZARUS   Tshotsholoza – tshotsholoza – yes I can, yes I can, yes I can.

GIBBS   *(Who has overheard approaches Lazarus and begins to imitate sound of train)* Yes I can, yes I can, yes I can.

DR ADDER   Gibbs!

GIBBS   *(Jumps)* Yessir, coming.

   Darkness.

SCENE IV

Lazarus is sitting in recreation room of asylum. He is wrapped in a blanket, seated in front of television with the sound off. Girl enters, she is half-caste in her teens. She wears a nightgown. She is thin and nervously attractive. She has a way of creating tension in a room and eventually taking it over. She carries a small transistor radio and is listening to music

JANETTE   That's my chair.

LAZARUS   Beg pardon?

JANETTE   That chair, it's mine. I always sit there.

LAZARUS   *(Moves to other chair)* Sorry.

JANETTE   *(She turns off the transistor, sits for a second, and then leaps from chair)* What's that? News? I hate news.

LAZARUS   You can change the – *(Sees that she already has)*

JANETTE   *(Sits for a second and then screams)* Boring! *(Looks at Lazarus with her cat eyes)* You the African?

LAZARUS   Sorry?

JANETTE   *(Mimicking him)* Sorry. What you sorry for? I asked you if you're the African.

LAZARUS   I guess so.

JANETTE   Shit, don't you know?

LAZARUS   Yes... I know.

JANETTE   What's the blanket for? You cold?

LAZARUS   No.

JANETTE   Then why you wearing a blanket, is that African?

LAZARUS   It keeps me...

JANETTE   Keeps you what?

LAZARUS   Warm.

JANETTE   What a wally. *(Pause)* You got a cigarette on you?

LAZARUS   No, sorry.

JANETTE   'Sorry.' *(Anticipates him and says it at the same time. She then takes out her own cigarettes)*

LAZARUS   *(Looks with disbelief and then laughs)* Oh!

JANETTE   What you staring at? You simple or just crazy? *(Crossing her legs which he can't help but look at)*

LAZARUS   Just trying.

JANETTE   Crying?

LAZARUS   Yes, crying and trying.

JANETTE   *(Looks, and then dismisses him)* Weird.

   Gibbs passing, sees her and enters

GIBBS   *(Singing)*
   Mona Lisa, Mona Lisa
   Men have named you

JANETTE   *(Calmly)* Fuck off.

GIBBS   *(To Lazarus)* I see you've met our Miss Janette. *(Turns back to Janette and pulls her ear)* Why your mouth so rude gal? Didn't I tell you, you mustn't speak to big people so?

JANETTE   Stop! *(Pushing hand away)*

GIBBS   You go get a cut-arse.

JANETTE   *(Sucks her teeth disdainfully)* Not by you, I won't.

GIBBS   Lazarus, give me your belt.

She stares at him with large, challenging eyes

GIBBS   How come you not getting dressed today?

JANETTE   I don't feel like it, that's why.

GIBBS   Slackness. You can't go around so. *(Paternal face)*

JANETTE   The Owl said I didn't have to dress. *(Crossing her legs again)* Anyway, you not my father.

GIBBS   Praise God for that. *(Pause)* But wait. You wearing anything under there at all?

JANETTE   Wouldn't you like to know.

GIBBS   *(To Lazarus)* Lazarus, this here is the razor queen. She try to chop a man neck off, ain't it, darling?

JANETTE   If it was you it wouldn't have been your neck.

GIBBS   *(Covering privates)* Rass! So doc say you don't have to get dress eh? You sure?

JANETTE   Go ask him.

GIBBS   I will. *(To Lazarus as he leaves)* Mind your neck.

Gibbs exits

JANETTE	Flunky! I hate him.
LAZARUS	You really... try to cut a man's throat?
JANETTE	Yeah, why not?
LAZARUS	*(Moves chair closer to her)* How did you feel?
JANETTE	When?
LAZARUS	When you cut his throat.
JANETTE	Wet.
LAZARUS	Wet? *(Pause)* You mean you were scared?
JANETTE	No, he was bleeding all over me.
LAZARUS	Oh. *(Moves back his chair)*
JANETTE	What are you here for?
LAZARUS	I'm not myself, so they say.
JANETTE	What did you do?
LAZARUS	I worked in the circus.
JANETTE	In the circus? Doing what?
LAZARUS	Tightrope walker.
JANETTE	So what happen?
LAZARUS	I fell off.
JANETTE	You never. I had a dream like that. Except it was on a ledge high up and there were people down below telling me to jump.
LAZARUS	And did you?
JANETTE	No, I never. Not even in my dream. *(Soft pause)* So what part of Africa you from then?
LAZARUS	The deep part.

JANETTE   What part's that?

LAZARUS   South Arica. Where the mines are. Loud births and still deaths.

JANETTE   You're lucky, at least you know who you are.

LAZARUS   Yeah I know, but I can't do anything about it.

JANETTE   My mother's white and my father's black.

LAZARUS   And their daughter?

JANETTE   I don't know what I am. That's why...

LAZARUS   Why what?

JANETTE   I don't know. Things just happen to me.

LAZARUS   Blessed was the fruit of thy mother's womb.

JANETTE   Oh yeah? She don't think so.

LAZARUS   And your father?

JANETTE   He don't exist as far as I'm concerned. If he ever tries to come near me again, I'll kill him.

LAZARUS   Like that guy who you chopped? *(Touching her)*

JANETTE   *(Screaming)* Don't touch me, right. I hate people touching me up. *(Steps away from him)*

LAZARUS   Sorry.

JANETTE   What am I bothering talking to you for?

LAZARUS   *(Seating himself and wrapping himself with blanket)* You know who you are girl. You may not like the word, but you know.

JANETTE   What word? *(He doesn't answer her. She runs*

over to where he sits and screams directly into his face) What word?

Dr Adder enters

DR ADDER   Janette, I think you should get dressed now, don't you?

JANETTE   *(Without looking at him)* I don't want to get dressed.

DR ADDER   Yes you do, dear.

JANETTE   No I don't. I don't want to get dressed, *dear*.

DR ADDER   *(Calm and snake-like)* All right then, you needn't get dressed, but that means you'll have to stay in your room.

JANETTE   No!

DR ADDER   Gibbs! *(Gibbs enters)* Show Janette to her room. Perhaps we'll see her for dinner.

GIBBS   *(Softly singing)*
Mona Lisa, Mona Lisa
Men have named you.

JANETTE   God, I hate you.

Janette exits with Gibbs

DR ADDER   A very emotional girl.

LAZARUS   What time is it?

DR ADDER   Five o'clock. Why? Not going somewhere are we?

LAZARUS   No, nothing. It's just the Wednesday matinee.

DR ADDER   Matinee?

LAZARUS   The show... I usually...

DR ADDER   Oh, the Boot Dance.

LAZARUS   You get into the habit of the show. You know, it's like the...

DR ADDER   Circus?

LAZARUS   *(Sudden shock, he wonders if this man has overheard him)* Yeah.

ADDER   You know, Lazarus, I think maybe you can't sleep because of guilt.

LAZARUS   Guilt? Me? You're crazy. You want to know why I don't sleep?

DR ADDER   Yes, why?

LAZARUS   It's because I don't trust sleep. Once, I went to sleep a prince and when I woke, I was a slave.

DR ADDER   That sounds like a child's fairy tale.

LAZARUS   To you maybe, but not to me. You see, the Zulu people, once we hunted the lion. Now we hunt jobs. *(The silence of the world)* You understand? All in the space of a dream.

DR ADDER   Well, at least you still hunt. Excuse me, will you?

Gibbs exits

LAZARUS   Trying not crying *(Soft pause)*. Trying.

He puts on an old trilby hat. He is seated on a chair and hums a South African chant to himself

God, this is like the way my father used to sit. His neck bent to the side like this *(Demonstrates)* listening to the wind in the corners of the evening. My mother would come and bring him his mealy

mealy. He only spoke on Saturdays, my father. The rest of the week he'd keep his own company, sucking on his pipe *(Mimes pipe – Pause)* Waiting for the world to behave.

Enter Gibbs

GIBBS   Hey Lazarus, I have a letter for you. *(He hands it to him)*

Lazarus looks at letter suspiciously then grabs it and tears it in half

GIBBS   You gonna eat it?... You all right?... What you want to do that for?

LAZARUS   They're just asking for help.

GIBBS   Well, the good thing about being crazy is that you don't have to send home money to your mother.

LAZARUS   Go on, then. Rush off to baas and report it.

GIBBS   What you think I am, a spy?

LAZARUS   Ha! *(Laughs)*

GIBBS   It's your business what you do with your mail. Most people here are glad to know what's going on outside.

LAZARUS   There is no outside, only in here.

GIBBS   Listen, my friend, there is an outside and it's full of piranha. Them that's not piranha are sharks.

LAZARUS   *(Looks at Gibbs quizzically and has a revelation)* You're the fisherman.

GIBBS   *(Doesn't understand so ignores it)* By the way, you think you could let me hold a few quid? Need little help until my ship comes in.

LAZARUS   What ship's that, the Titanic?

GIBBS   A six-horse race. A sure thing.

LAZARUS   You want me to give you money for a horse race?

GIBBS   Communication problem. I want you to help me with an investment.

LAZARUS   Investment?

GIBBS   Yeah, in my future. My immediate future.

LAZARUS   Sorry, friend.

GIBBS   Come on, what good it doing you, burning a hole in your pocket?

LAZARUS   Better my pocket than the bookie's.

GIBBS   Boy, you Africans hard. I don't know which is worse, a Jew or an African. One is stone, the next is iron.

LAZARUS   Yeah, well at least we know how to keep it once we get it.

GIBBS   Cha, to raas! Well, maybe a West Indian would tief your drawers, but only an African would try to sell it back to you.

LAZARUS   What you know about Africans?

GIBBS   Plenty. I knew one who try and sell his own mother a tombstone but she dead before he could collect. *(Soft pause)* So he write her name on one side and his own on the next and then drop dead out of spite.

LAZARUS   Here! *(Gives him a pound)*

GIBBS   *(Aside)* Tight like a duck's ass.

LAZARUS   What?

GIBBS   Thanks, it's a start.

LAZARUS   Gibbs, you ever win?

GIBBS   It's not the winning, it's the playing. I won't lie. I love horse. A horse is a clean animal. There's not a part of it you can't use for something. Different to a man. Even the shit from a horse, you could make something grow. *(Child eyes)* I wish to God I could own one, but I'm not in them league. I have to make do with racetrack.

LAZARUS   So you're not just a gambler, you're a sportsman.

GIBBS   You call it what you want. I just know that from small I see my father work like a donkey. You hear me, not a horse, because a horse have some style. No, he work like a donkey, building the Panama Canal. When night come he would be too tired to go shit. He would fall asleep in his clothes. Yes man, my father, the donkey.

LAZARUS   Sounds like my father. He worked the mines.

GIBBS   So you see, a horse not like that. It have a history, a pedigree, I mean. Say it was sired by Red Rum or Shergar. You know what I mean? If you just a man, a Smith, a Jones, a Gibbs, you may as well go dead. That's why in my next life I coming back as a horse. Hell, even a good dog got better chance than a man. Well, next time I'll know better.

LAZARUS   What? You think you're going to come again?

GIBBS   Why not? I come before, no reason to think he go let me off now.

LAZARUS   Who?

GIBBS   Master God. He give me a few centuries of lash in me backside, but I reckon I still have couple more to go. *(Looks at Lazarus and smiles, the smile of the conspirator)* You too.

LAZARUS   What... What have I done wrong? I mean, what sin could make me have to...

GIBBS   *Us*, make us.

LAZARUS   All right, us.

GIBBS   Well, sin is a funny kind of word, you know. Say *stupidness*. That make more sense.

LAZARUS   Stupidness?

GIBBS   Yeah. You see, once upon a time we had paradise, and our life was sweet, too sweet. Every damn thing we want was there to our hand. Food, women, the rhythm of life, but we didn't know what to do with it. Too much joy, too much which was gladness.

Then God sent the white man, dry and cold like ice. And because the drum was too loud for his ear, he invented the clock, because, you see, the white man's drum *is* the clock. And he divided up the day into twelve hours of work, and he say: 'Okay you fuckers, I go show you what time is for. God chose you to suffer and me to rule.'

LAZARUS   Labour, like the donkey, like the goat.

GIBBS   Turn the land into an emeny. You think you working it but it working you. And now even your woman is war. Just like the land. She come a stranger. So you now, you try and drink your way back to paradise because somewhere in your mind you can remember something better. But drink not enough and smoke not enough. So is now you want Paradise, and you know why? Because it blood claat gone.

LAZARUS   The world dances on your face and calls it history.

GIBBS   Cho, let me go and do my rounds.

Gibbs exits

Lazarus gets down on floor and pieces together torn letter. Gibbs re-enters and finds Lazarus reading aloud

LAZARUS   Your father is dead.

GIBBS   You praying? No praying allowed here.

LAZARUS   No, I was just... cleaning the floor.

GIBBS   Oh well, that's all right then. Everything correct.

Gibbs exits laughing

LAZARUS   Zu dilike intaba! Inkosi ye lizwe inshonile. Your father is dead. *(Tears in his eyes)* Everything correct *(Slowly takes off his father's trilby hat)*

Darkness

SCENE V – Study for girl with beads

Janette is in the day room dancing to the reggae beat which comes from a tape deck. ('Moulding' by I. Jah Man Levi.) She is dressed in jeans and T-shirt, which shows her body to good advantage. Her mood is in total contrast to early scene. Dr Adder enters and watches her for some time, unnoticed. She holds a letter in her hand as she dances

DR ADDER   Well, Janette, you seem in a better mood. Had some good news, have we?

JANETTE   Well, you should know, you read all my bloody mail, don't you?

DR ADDER   Of course not. It's not the done thing.

JANETTE   Well, *you* done it.

DR ADDER   Don't be silly.

JANETTE   Oh, paranoid am I?

DR ADDER   Perhaps just a bit.

JANETTE   Perhaps just a bit? You like watching inside my head?

DR ADDER   Not watching, *looking* I should have said.

JANETTE   Yeah, that's why you come searching-up my room and that.

DR ADDER   I've never done any searching.

JANETTE   So who does it then? If he does, it's on your orders.

DR ADDER   My dear child, I've never given any such orders, I can assure you.

JANETTE   Go on, assure me.

DR ADDER   Believe me.

JANETTE   Then how come my things are always turned upside down, my drawers and that?

DR ADDER   I couldn't tell you. I'll make enquiries.

JANETTE   You do that.

DR ADDER *(Turning away)* I had hoped... you thought of me as a friend.

JANETTE A friend?

DR ADDER Well, at least not an enemy.

JANETTE Oh yeah, what's that going to cost?

DR ADDER Cost? Cost who, Janette?

JANETTE Me and all?

DR ADDER Why, nothing.

JANETTE When men say *nothing*, that means it's *really* going to cost.

DR ADDER You came to me for help.

JANETTE I didn't come, I was sent.

DR ADDER Well, in any case, it's my duty to do all I possibly can for you –

JANETTE By spying on me?

DR ADDER You know, in some ways you remind me of my daughter.

Dr Adder tries to touch her when Gibbs enters

GIBBS Telephone for you, guvnor.

DR ADDER Thank you. Excuse me.

Dr Adder exits to phone

JANETTE What are you staring at?

GIBBS Something sweet.

JANETTE You not getting any of it. *(She starts to dance)*

GIBBS *(Pointing at letter)* Boyfriend?

JANETTE   No, *girlfriend. (Challenging)*

GIBBS   Oh, too bad. What a waste of talent.

> *They laugh together. Gibbs begins to dance beside her. She ignores him. He moves in the slow suggestive manner of the Calypso*

JANETTE   Old style.

GIBBS   It may be old, but it's still style. Me could still show you something.

JANETTE   *(Suddenly stopping the music)* That's the way my father used to dance.

GIBBS   *(Looking at her in surprise)* So, that's the way my father dance. What wrong with that?

JANETTE   I don't like it.

GIBBS   What's your problem, girl? Is like you have a bee in your ass.

JANETTE   You play the horses, don't you?

GIBBS   Yeah. So?

JANETTE   And the pools. And you drink your rum from Friday night to Monday morning.

> *Lazarus enters. Gibbs notices him*

You married?

GIBBS   Yes, girl.

JANETTE   How many children you got?

GIBBS   Why?

JANETTE   And you probably got three or four more all over the place. Tell me, what you gonna tell your wife's kids when you decide to bring the others to live with you? 'Listen here then, picnies, these are your new brothers and sisters.'

GIBBS   Look, is not me your father girl. Me never blow in your mother ear. Don't blame me.

JANETTE   *(Changes mood)* Today's my birthday. *(Gibbs looks at her bewildered)* Today is my birthday.

GIBBS   Oh yeah. Happy birthday.

JANETTE   What are you going to give me?

GIBBS   Give you?

JANETTE   Yeah, for my birthday.

GIBBS   It depends.

JANETTE   On what?

GIBBS   On how my luck goes. What time is it?

JANETTE   *(Looking at watch)* Half two.

GIBBS   Shit. The race.

Gibbs exits

JANETTE   Christ on a bike, what a place to have to spend a birthday.

LAZARUS   Is it really your birthday?

JANETTE   Yes. What you going to give me?

Lazarus goes over to her and, taking the beads from his neck, places them around hers

LAZARUS   Here.

JANETTE   I was just messing about. You don't have to. I mean, this is yours.

LAZARUS   I wanted to give you something. That's all I have right now. It's easy enough for a birthday.

JANETTE   And what do you want?

LAZARUS   What I want, you can't give me.

JANETTE   *(Fingering beads)* You're different. People like him *(Pointing in the direction of Gibbs' exit)* will just take as long as there's taking and then bugger off. Just like my father. They leave you with glass and cut wrists. *(Pause)* I know them. My mother used to sit screaming in her room surrounded by her dolls.

LAZARUS   Your mother?

JANETTE   Yeah. I thought women were built to handle pain. She couldn't.

LAZARUS   Maybe that's what she wanted.

JANETTE   No, she just wanted to get away from English tea and those houses all alike with the knickers stretched out on a line in the yard. *(Pause)* And when she'd walk through the streets with this black man so close everyone stared at them. My grandmother was Catholic. You can imagine, she did her nut.

LAZARUS   No, they don't forgive that, the English. Though they smile. All teeth and chat and curtains at the window... *(Pause)* ... but they never forget.

JANETTE   *(Doing their voices)*
'You're that little Wilson girl, then. Your father's the coloured fellow, right? What's become of him, then?'
'Gone away.'
'Oh, doing time is he?'
'No, just doing without us.'
'Shame. About your mother, I mean. Still, I

wonder why they do it?'
'To get away. *(Pause)* Away.

Janette exits. Lazarus is left alone again.

Darkness

SCENE VI

Lazarus is alone in his room. He is troubled. He stares at his boots. The silence is heavy. He is very depressed. He starts crying. To try and pull himself together he hums a song. The humming develops into singing. Then he realizes he is singing his father's favourite song and stops. He walks about the room. Slowly he decides to do the Boot Dance again. He puts the boots on. If he can do it again and not break down he will be able to leave this place, to be free. Very slowly he starts to dance. He is unsteady, unsure. Voices start to build. Not voices, laughter. The laughter is frightening, taunting. People, the audience, find him comical, quaint, exotic. They know that as a black person he can never make a living out of the Boot Dance. Lazarus cannot stop the laughter. Unseen by Lazarus, Janette is coming to see him. She stops when she sees what is happening. He tries to shout, but nothing comes out – it's like someone is trying to strangle him, and he can't breathe. The laughter stops abruptly. Janette watches discreetly, silently. She is amazed; she slips away. Lazarus slowly regains control, takes off his boots, puts them in a corner, sits and looks at them for a long beat

Darkness

ACT 2

SCENE I – The Touch

Monday of third week: Lazarus is alone on stage. Gibbs enters with morning cup of coffee and the Sporting Life

LAZARUS You late, you know, Gibbs.

GIBBS I know I'm late.

LAZARUS We can't have that. Guards can't be late.

GIBBS So what happen now? Me must give you account for my time?

LAZARUS Tsk tsk. Slackness!

GIBBS What? Cho... You mad out you ass. Talking to you is like talking to meself. *(Continues drinking coffee and checking horses)*

LAZARUS Right, I'm mad. Mad! Mad!

GIBBS *(Ignores him)* Hmm. Tell you boy, talk about bad luck. Of all the trains in London to jump in front of, this guy have to choose mine.

LAZARUS Which guy?

GIBBS Some damn fool. You would expect an Englishman to have better manners. But no. No kind of consideration. You wouldn't do something like that, would you? I mean, look at it. People them going to work, nice fresh newspapers folded in they laps. Head still bad from the night before. Wife in you arse, landlord in you arse, boss in you arse. And here comes this fellow now, jump down on the track, right into the middle of everybody's life. Jesus! People them was vex. They jaws tight.

LAZARUS   Damn inconsiderate.

GIBBS   Right. Killing yourself should be like going toilet. Should be done in private. You don't want mash-up people business. By the time they cleaned him off the walls, I was an hour and a half late. *(Sips coffee and checks horses)*

LAZARUS   What would you have done, Gibbs?

GIBBS   Me? Well, if I want kill meself I would stay home in me yard. Might as well, just as cheap. Fire back two drinks, play little music, *(Pause)* check to make sure me wearing some clean drawers and that it don't have no holes. Gentleman.

LAZARUS   Of course.

GIBBS   Well, you don't want people talking after you any, and anyhow my mother always used to say...

LAZARUS   But how would you do it?

GIBBS   Do what?

LAZARUS   Kill yourself.

GIBBS   Oh well, I'd fire back two drinks...

LAZARUS   You said that.

GIBBS   Then I'd listen to all my music one last time.

Pause, he stands

LAZARUS   *(Angrily)* But how would you kill yourself?

GIBBS   You know, to tell the truth, when that rhythm start to hold me *(Starts to wind his waist)* cho, boy, I wouldn't dead just yet. Life hard for true, but no man, me could make *one* more day. *Always*. No, I'm not your man for suicide, sorry.

Lazarus relaxes and sings a Zulu praise song – 'Babulala Maqawe', 'they kill the heroes'

What that is?

LAZARUS   It says, my father is dead. His cattle and his land is mine. Long live my father's son. *(Pause)* But my father *is* dead, Gibbs. And there is no land and no cattle. And all he's left me is his shadow. I can't even go home to bury him.

GIBBS   *(Turning away)* Well, my father dead, and so?

LAZARUS   At least you can go home.

GIBBS   Go home? Says you. I can't go home, poor brother.

LAZARUS   You know what apartheid is?

GIBBS   Sure I know.

LAZARUS   They gave me a one way ticket out.

GIBBS   Shit, you lucky you get a ticket. I had was to tief mine.

LAZARUS   I can't even go home to bury my father.

GIBBS   Well, somebody soon bury him when he stink too bad.

LAZARUS   From the cradle to the grave they control us. They tell us when to die or where. And who to call father.

GIBBS   Listen, my friend, make me tell you about the Caribbean. We suppose to be free, right? Not a white man suppose to be in charge anywhere unless you look inside a telephone or under a flag,

right? But me let them catch me walking along certain beach or outside one of them tourist hotel or sports club and its rass to pay. Police! *(Mimics voices)*
'What you doing here, boy, you work here?'
'Well, no sir.'
'Well, you not a guest. You can't pay all them kind of one and two hundred dollar a day business, so what you doing here? You come to clean out the shit?'
'No sir.'
'Well then, is tief you must be. Come to tief?'
'Listen, this is my country. Is here I born, you know.'
'Oh yes?'
Wham, wham, two quick lick in you ass and here come a boot to you ballocks. You know how easy it is to dead in the Caribbean? To vanish from this earth without a soul asking questions except you mother or you child? Dead from police. Dead from soldier.

LAZARUS   But you have a home. A passport. A country.

GIBBS   Bullshit! Any bloodclaat white man could come my island and live like a god, you understand. No matter if he drunk until he chupid. Anything happen to him is embassy, queen, prime minister, president, all kind of rass. But me now, who born there, could dead like a dog and only the sea know. And that thing hurt me, you hear sir. So now you come tell me, what is apartheid?

Gibbs reaches hand to Lazarus. The silence of the world between them. They touch

Darkness

SCENE II – The Game of Bowls

One day later. Dr Adder's office. 'La Bohème' by Puccini is playing on Adder's cassette player. As scene opens Dr Adder is seen setting up a game of bowls on his office floor. He slowly and methodically sends the ball across, lifting his back foot like a bird, and then urges it on. He then applauds himself by clapping the back of his left hand with the front of his right. Janette enters and stares at him for a moment. He turns and sees her. She wears a dress

DR ADDER   Ah yes, Janette, come in, come in. *(He puts on jacket)* Sit. I hear you attacked Gibbs. Not nice. Here we don't attack guards.

JANETTE   Don't you want to hear my side... *(Adder points finger)* Okay, okay. No attack Gibbs.

DR ADDER   Right, no attack Gibbs.

JANETTE   When do you think I can go home?

DR ADDER   *(Comes over to her and begins to finger the beads she is wearing, looking at them in his near-sighted way)* Very nice, very nice.

JANETTE   So when do you think?

DR ADDER   Tell me, Janette, when you ran away from home was it to hurt your mother or your father?

JANETTE   I didn't want to hurt anybody. I just couldn't take it any more. The whole situation.

DR ADDER   When you say situation –

JANETTE   Things were bad enough before, but when my father came back it just got bloody ridiculous. I told my mother, 'look, the guy's just using you.' Five years we didn't have a word from him.

Flipping hell, five years, nothing, he just pissed off and left us. Nobody knew if he was in prison or what. Then all of a sudden he shows up one day, just like that. Just like nothing ever happened.

DR ADDER   And so what did your mother do?

JANETTE   What did she do? She takes him back. I said, 'mum, don't be stupid, he's just going to do the same thing all over again. We don't need him. We're doing all right as we are. What do you want him for?'
She says, 'you're young, you don't understand these things.'
She just let him come in and take over. A right little king he is. He just sits in front of the telly like this. *(She imitates him)* When I left school I get this job in the factory pressing clothes on this machine, right. Now if they ever catch you sitting down, that's it, they chop you. All flipping day you're on your feet. Just blacks and Greeks and a few Filipinos with dead eyes. So by the time I come home, I'm really knackered, right? All I want to do is fall down on the floor and rest my back. Do you know, that bastard expected me to serve him his dinner. I said, 'look mate, maybe mom's your slave, but not me.'

DR ADDER   I take it he didn't like that.

JANETTE   He went mad. Slapped me around. I think he would have killed me if mom didn't come home then.

DR ADDER   And so did she do anything at that point?

JANETTE   You're joking. Do anything? Mom? She never does anything except cry. 'Well, you've got to remember he's still your father.' What father? I don't even know him, he's been gone for five years. I know the bloody grocer better than I know my father. I said, 'Look mum, you're screwing him at night, not me. You have to take all this shit, not me. As long as he's in this house you're not going to see me, right. So you choose.'

DR ADDER   And did she?

JANETTE   I did it for her. I left. I left them to whatever little happiness they thought they could get away with. But it soon came apart again.

DR ADDER   Why?

JANETTE   Well, he went off again, didn't he? And she ... cut her wrist, trying to spite him. Stupid bitch. As if he cared.

DR ADDER   I shouldn't put it quite like that, Janette.

JANETTE   She is a stupid bitch. To think that it would make any difference to a rat like him. I thought they said people are supposed to get wiser when they get old.

DR ADDER   It sometimes doesn't work quite that way.

JANETTE   You think I would ever be dumb enough to kill myself for some man?

DR ADDER   Well, maybe you'll be lucky and some man will kill himself for you one day.

JANETTE   *(Slowly)* When I came in the house the place was full of smoke. She had left a pot on the fire. I went into the kitchen and turned it off. I heard the telly in the living room. I called her but she didn't answer. Then I saw the light on in my room. The place was covered in blood and broken glass. She was laying across my bed. But why did she have to choose my room to do it? I still can't understand. She had the whole apartment and she chooses my friggin' room. I felt sick.

I called the police and the ambulance and they took forever to come. When they finally came they kept asking all these stupid questions. 'Why did she do it?' How do I know why? Just take her to the hospital, will you? The telly was on and the guy kept looking at it. Game for a Laugh.

I tried to clean up my room but I couldn't. In the end I just threw all the sheets and bedclothes away. I wanted to burn everything. I swear I'll never go back there again. The room smells like death.

DR ADDER   But she lived, didn't she?

JANETTE   Yes, she's alive.

DR ADDER   You then attacked your father with a knife?

JANETTE   Yeah, I meant to –

DR ADDER   To kill him?

JANETTE   Yeah, I should of done.

DR ADDER   Janette, we can't go around killing parents.

JANETTE   Why not? They go around killing us, don't they? If they get the chance. By the time they get done with you, it's a wonder there's anything left. Who has a better right to kill them?

DR ADDER   Interesting way of looking at it, but I'm afraid the law doesn't approve of patricide, it's bad for taxes.

JANETTE   Well, when can I leave here?

DR ADDER   It depends.

JANETTE   On what?

DR ADDER   On you, really.

JANETTE   No it doesn't, it depends on what you say. You're the doctor.

DR ADDER   You know, Janette, even we can't always do what we like to.

JANETTE   Why?

DR ADDER   My responsibility is to try and make certain that you're safe for society.

JANETTE   Safe for society?

DR ADDER   Yes. I'm afraid you have to be a little more... ashamed of what you've done.

JANETTE   Okay, I'm ashamed. I'm ashamed. I didn't know what I was doing.

DR ADDER   Not quite. Let's give it a little more time, shall we?

JANETTE   You mean I'm not sorry enough yet?

DR ADDER   *(Touching her)* I have something for you. *(A child's smile on an old man's face)* A present.

JANETTE   Present?

DR ADDER   *(Taking box from desk and pausing before giving it to her)* Here, open it.

JANETTE   *(Looks at him and then opens box nervously)* Shoes...

DR ADDER   Let me do it.

He gets down on knees and very gently places the shoes on her feet. They are very delicate evening shoes with straps. It is evident that he spent some time choosing them

I know that your right foot is a little larger than your left.

JANETTE   How did you – ?

DR ADDER   I noticed. *(Fastens straps)* There! I didn't want the heels too high. They must be just *(Pause)* right.

Gibbs knocks and enters. Sees Adder

GIBBS   Backside! Sorry... I'll come back. *(Aside)* This should be well sweet. Me feel say, doctor want to eat the cherry but can't reach the tree.

Gibbs exits

DR ADDER   *(Trying to stand on leg which has gone to sleep)* There comes a time when the body has its little mutiny.

JANETTE   You all right? *(Helps him into chair)*

DR ADDER   Fine, fine. *(Rubbing leg)* Just a little revolt. Let me see you walk in them.

JANETE   Yes? *(She parades a little for him)*

DR ADDER   Lovely, simply lovely.

JANETTE   Thank you. Can I go now?

DR ADDER   Go? Yes, yes, by all means.

Janette exits. Dr Adder places the tissue paper very meticulously inside the shoe box and closes it. Hums a bit from aria: 'La donna e mobile'

Slow darkness

SCENE III

Lazarus seated in the day room with Gibbs. He is looking at photographs of himself when he first came to England

LAZARUS   That's when I first came.

GIBBS   Hey, you really look young in this one. See the boy in suit and tie. Look like you going communion. *(Laughs)*

LAZARUS   Trying to figure it out. Trying to remember. The eyes... see the eyes different. Everything open, exposed. I believed, you see. I thought it was all over. Thought I'd won, coming here... When I'd walk into a room, I'd come in too quick.

GIBBS   How you mean?

LAZARUS   It was like my spirit would enter first, too full. They don't like that. White people here are like... I don't know, they're always on neutral. Perpetual neutral. I could feel them backing off or tilting away.

You see, back home, when you greet a man, you *greet* him. You greet his family, you greet his hope, yes? You hug him. *(He hugs Gibbs)* That way you feel his strength, give him some of yours, feel his spirit. *(Pause)* But here... it's like death slips in between and you can see it there in a man's face when you look. Like a wound so you don't look. You never look. So I learned how to go on neutral like them. How to laugh at things that aren't funny. How to never expect. And, above all, how to never call sadness by its name. They wear out your dreams, man, but still they don't let you in. Secret, they never let you in. *(Turns suddenly)* Look at him!

GIBBS   *(Looks, not understanding what is happening)* Who?

LAZARUS   That's Lazarus, he's been here a long time now. He's not raw any more. His blood must have gotten thin by now.

GIBBS   Your blood gets thin in this cold, yes.

LAZARUS   There's other blacks coming over. The marks of the whip still fresh on their backs. Let's try them. I don't think he can cry any more. He can't do the Boot Dance *(Pause)* any more. He can't –

GIBBS   You see, these English people here, they *hungry*, you hear me. Never mind how they prance and parade like everything going sweet. They catching hell. Is hungry them hungry, so the serious business they must keep for themselves, always. And so you now, you will have to make do with the afters. Now, you look at the bulldog. When he bite he can't let go because he got lockjaw. If you die, he dies, but he *can't* let go, *ever*.

Janette enters carrying her cassette. Music playing (Stevie Wonder: From 'Innervisions' – 'Don't you worry 'bout a thing', followed by 'He's Mister Know it all'. Gibbs eyes her

GIBBS   I see you get a next present.

JANETTE   Gibbs, do me a favour. When you see me, right?

GIBBS   Yeah?

JANETTE   Don't see me.

GIBBS   Fair enough.

LAZARUS   What's the matter?

JANETTE   Nothing's the matter, I'm just insane, didn't you know. Bonkers. Not safe for society. Card carrying crazy.

LAZARUS   You're not crazy. I know about crazy.

JANETTE   Yeah, well, he says I am, and he's got the power right.

LAZARUS   What do you want, Janette?

JANETTE   I want to get the hell out of here, that's what I want.

LAZARUS   And then what?

JANETTE   What do you mean, and then what? Life.

LAZARUS   Oh yeah, that's still happening, right. I forgot.

JANETTE   That's right, it's happening, and I can deal with it, all of it.

LAZARUS   Anyhow and any way.

JANETTE   Let's have a party.

GIBBS   What?

JANETTE   My party. Invite everybody.

LAZARUS   Something to drink.

JANETTE   Yeah. Gibbs?

They look at him

GIBBS   What you expect me to buy it?

LAZARUS   Here. *(Giving money)*

GIBBS   I'm going to have to ask The Owl.

JANETTE   It's all right, you go ask him.

GIBBS   I soon come.

Gibbs exits. Janette starts to dance, Lazarus joins her

LAZARUS   Give me some of your strength.

JANETTE   Strength? Me?

LAZARUS   You're sure, the way I used to be. You believe that when you wake up in the morning life is still going to be there. And it is. Give me some of your woman's strength.

Janette looks at him. She holds him and they dance

JANETTE   Listen, you know what you have to do to get around them, people like Adder?

LAZARUS   What?

JANETTE   You've got to confess to them, a little at a time. They like to feel like they're getting to know you. White people, I mean. You don't have to feel better, just act like you do. That way they leave you alone. Just don't let them do you. Break your spirit like they did my dad.

LAZARUS   I thought you hated him.

JANETTE   It's not that I hate him, right? I hate what he let them do to him. You just don't let them waste you too. My mother always said he really wanted to punch God, except she was closer.

SCENE IV

Flashback. Lazarus does a brief chant of melancholy. He comes in, sits down, head between knees as if exhausted. Looks up as if seeing someone

LAZARUS Hey Lucky, I want to see you. No, no, I'm not going to the pub tonight. Every day before the show – the pub. After the show the pub. Give the pub a rest for a minute, hey? Nothing's wrong. I'm tired, you know, that's all. *(Pause)*

Look, one of these days the show is going to close. Come on, man, it can't last forever. Nothing is forever... Don't be stupid, I'm not bringing bad luck.

Wo! Ngi hudelwa yi hubulu.

I'm just speaking facts. One day it will all be over, then what? Don't you ever think about it? No, you're too busy in the pub.

What?... I'm not putting you down. Look, all I'm... *(Shouts)* I'm not putting you down, Lucky! I'm just saying, use your head, man. We're here in England. How many years we've been away from home? How many? This white woman, this Miss Peggy does all the talking for us. She holds the passports, she pays the salaries, she gives all the interviews –

Will you wait? Let me finish. All right, she's been like a bloody mother to us but I've already got a mother. I don't need another one. I think it's time we looked after ourselves, yeah, go off on our own. *(Pause)*

Why? Why not? This isn't South Africa any more, it's supposed to be bloody England, remember. We don't need anybody to speak for us. If we still can't do what we want then what's the sense? What did we come for?

Where's the achievement? Where's the freedom? Okay, we get to fuck a few white women. Sula

izembe, wipe our axes dry. *(Makes a sign of copulation)* Great! Is that what it was all about? No, man. Now we trek across a new desert, America, England, to Germany, to Holland, to Sweden, and back to England again. Keep going in a circle. Keep out of the way of the police because we're just guests of the government. Be seen, but don't see. And at night we try to trick our bodies to sleep – but we're dying, man. For what, Lucky, for what? *(Sees his friend is impatient)* It's all right, man. Go on, you'll be late for the pub.
No, no, go on; Drink, man, drink.

(Holds boots in his hands) We're not dancing; it's dancing us. *(Drops boots)*

SCENE V – The Children of the Eighth Day

Dr Adder is listening to the overture from 'Die Fledermaus' by Johann Strauss. Lazarus enters Dr Adder's office. He drops photographs on desk

LAZARUS   Whatever happened to him?

DR ADDER   What's this *(Looking nearsightedly at picture)* Why, it's you, isn't it? ... Nice, very nice photo.

LAZARUS   But whatever happened to him, that boy?

DR ADDER   Well, what happens to any of us? He just became a man, *(Looking at him)* or did he?

LAZARUS   No, they killed him.

DR ADDER   Sometimes you have to kill the boy to reach the man. Now, I have something to show you. I have this book, my telephone book. *(Takes out small black book)* You know what I call it? My X directory. And you know why? Because most of the people in it are dead, my contemporaries. *(Shows him)* You see the Xs? The reason I do that is because things have a habit of dropping out of my head lately. Little pieces of the brain, memory mostly. I forget and call people up at night and someone answers and says: 'Sorry, but I died. Don't you remember coming to the funeral?' And I say: 'Ah yes... so you did.' *(Pause)* Not that I mind, you understand, but it's very annoying to be reminded all the time.

LAZARUS   Reminded of what?

DR ADDER   That you're dying. *(Pause)* Death has a nasty habit of buggering you long before you're ready for it. I'm sorry, I have no placebos, no little instant pain removers. But let's have some tea, eh? Where there's tea –

LAZARUS   – there's hope. You know the only difference between here and South Africa? In South Africa they play with your body, they play with terror. Here they play with your mind. They use the forceps on your brain. They pull it this way, then that. They've got a million ways to say 'no'. They specialize in playing with your hope, that part of you that dreams.

DR ADDER   Who do you love, Lazarus?

LAZARUS   Love, what are you talking about? Love?

DR ADDER   Love. Do you love anyone?

LAZARUS   I don't have anything left over.

DR ADDER   I don't understand.

LAZARUS   Look, I came over here to work. Dance. Music. That's what I do – when they let me. There's nothing else.

DR ADDER   But did you feel anything for anyone?

LAZARUS   What the hell are you talking about, feel anything? Tired man, that's all, tired! You don't understand, these people make you work for it.

DR ADDER   For what?

LAZARUS   For nothing, for nothing at all but they still make you work for it. Just to live. It's like they make you cut a switch to beat your own backside with. So you see, I don't have anything left over to love with. I've been running too hard.

DR ADDER   Well, then, if you don't love anything, what's the point? Who do you trust?

LAZARUS   I don't trust anybody, I can't afford it.

DR ADDER   My friend, nine out of every ten people are in the same situation, only they call it life. You don't have any mates from back home, do you?

LAZARUS   *(Shock of recognition)* What about them? They just want to get together and talk about South Africa. *(Shouts)* I'm not in South Africa, I'm in fucking England. Here's where I am, and I'm dying. Right here. But nobody wants to talk about that because it hurts more here.

DR ADDER   Why?

LAZARUS   Because back there you don't expect. Here you lie. They lied. Everyone lies.

DR ADDER   Who lied?

LAZARUS   You. You said there was a chance. You said things would be different here. Tshotsholoza – yes I can, yes I can, yes I can – Tshukshuku – Tshukshuku – the train is coming but it never quite comes, always and ever in the land of 'almost'.

DR ADDER   The land of 'almost'?

LAZARUS   Yeah, and God is very patient when it comes to us. He doesn't mind waiting forever. Making us wait.

DR ADDER   What if I told you that I was no stranger to suffering?

LAZARUS   No, you specialize in it. Other people's.

DR ADDER   You don't think the Jews have known suffering? I could tell you stories...

LAZARUS   The Jews have some place; it's something different with us. We're the children of the eighth day.

DR ADDER   The eighth day?

LAZARUS   Seven-eighths of Africa is free, we're the last. You understand, the very last. They say the Lord built the world in six days and then he rested, right?

DR ADDER   Right.

LAZARUS   Well, it's been a long rest day. We're still waiting on the eighth day.

DR ADDER   Go to Ninevah, that great city, and cry against it.

LAZARUS   I don't know Ninevah, boss, but I know Soweto. I know KwaZulu. We're the only people that they never will forgive.

DR ADDER   Never forgive?

LAZARUS   For fighting. They will never forgive that, not for another thousand years. It's because they've seen us on our feet, they make sure that we stay on our knees.

DR ADDER   It takes two to play slavery, Lazarus. *(Mocking and taunting laughter starts, and builds quickly, and stops abruptly for Lazarus to say his next line – all the sounds are in his mind)* Both have to agree. If one doesn't agree, well then...

LAZARUS   So then it's just a game according to you.

DR ADDER   Well, there are games and games, but if you understand the psychology of oppression –

Lazarus grabs him about the neck and takes a letter-opener to his throat

LAZARUS   All right, analyze this, doctor. I want your home, I want your land, I want your labour, I want your God.

DR ADDER   *(Begins to scream)* Careful!

LAZARUS   What do you say?

DR ADDER   All right, all right.

LAZARUS   Say yes baas.

DR ADDER   Yes, yes baas.

LAZARUS   And I want your father.

DR ADDER   My father?

LAZARUS   Say 'yes, baas' *(Pricks him with knife)*... Got Kaffir, jo moor.

DR ADDER   My father, yes, baas... yes, baas.

LAZARUS   *(Releases him slowly, sits down in chair)* Good. Just a game. The psychology of what?

DR ADDER   *(Feeling his throat)* Oppression.

Gibbs enters

GIBBS   *(Looking at Dr Adder who is staring at Lazarus)*

Doctor, Janette is gone.

They turn to him in unison

DR ADDER   What?! Check the entire hospital. We must get her back. If you let her get away, I swear, Gibbs, I'll... I'll...

GIBBS   It wasn't my fault.

DR ADDER   Notify the police. C'mon, Gibbs, right away. *(Exit Gibbs) (To Lazarus)* Now, you, Lazarus – one thing is clear, one thing is definitely clear – you're not safe for society yet, oh no. We'll have to keep you here a little bit longer. Give you time to exercise some control over your actions. Still too wild and violent at the moment, I'm afraid.

Adder is still feeling his throat. Lazarus walks out of the office as lights fade out

SCENE VI

Gibbs enters Lazarus's room; he seems slightly bent, slightly discarded. Lazarus is singing

GIBBS   Well, them fire me.

LAZARUS   Fired you?

GIBBS   Ten years, and them fire me just so, like it was nothing. Ten years. Would of soon be eleven, April come, and them fire me easy as piss.

LAZARUS   What did they say?

GIBBS   Say I wasn't at my post. I went out put a bet on. But I wasn't gone for more than ten minutes or so. Is that damn girl fault, you know? I bet you she do it for spite. She know I go out at half two so that's why she time it so. Shit, a man can't guard all the time. I mean, even the devil does sleep.

LAZARUS   She had to get away.

GIBBS   Well, I glad for her, but why she couldn't do it at night when somebody else on duty? Damn girl is a problem. All now so I can hear she laughing. You don't worry about her. She's a mulatto. She still the colour of hope. She will always get by. We the colour of truth, that's why we catch licks. Here, take this. *(Gives him a pound)*

LAZARUS   What's this for?

GIBBS   Me horse got through. You can't lose all the time.

LAZARUS   *(Shock)* You're paying me back?

GIBBS   Money not my god, is the white man that let it mad him. *(Pause)* How about you now?

LAZARUS   Me?

GIBBS   Are you religious?

LAZARUS   Not at the moment.

GIBBS   When do you plan on leaving this place?

LAZARUS   I'm not ready to deal with that yet.

GIBBS   So when you go ready? Is like you love asylum. Enough black men in this madhouse. It well easy to get in, is leaving the problem.

LAZARUS   Look, I can't handle it yet.

GIBBS   So when?

LAZARUS   When it gets easier.

GIBBS *(Laughing)* Man, it don't get easier, you just get *deader*. That's all.

LAZARUS So how...

GIBBS One foot at a time, just like you putting on you pants. You try and do both together, you fall on your arse. But first you must *want* to come out.

LAZARUS *(Holding Gibbs)* Want to come out? It's the *wanting* that got me here. Listen, I did a lot of things to a lot of people to get away... to come to this country. *(Turning away)* And for what? Just to break into a fucking madhouse? My father said if I danced well, they would forgive my blackness.

GIBBS *(Sees the tears in Lazarus's eyes)* Forgive your blackness? Boy, that's gonna take a whole heap of dancing. Well, not to worry. With the grace of God you'll get a next chance to fuck-up, or to save a few more lives before you're dead. *(West Indian smile of teeth)* Them say truth does be bitter. When you black there's only two ways they forgive you for living: genius and money. Well, since them only give you 'genius' when you dead, I guess it's going to have to be money. I gone. *(Takes off his guard's jacket and places it on Lazarus's shoulders)* Wait a minute. *(Checks jacket pocket for money)* Right. Walk good. *(Throws keys to Lazarus)* May you find water in your well. *(Pause)* Instead of piss.

Gibbs exits

Sound of 'Meditations', John Coltrane. The stage is flooded with light. The rising of the dead son now united with father

LAZARUS 'One foot at a time.' *(Pauses, looks at keys)* When I was a child I cried and my mother came.

Then, when I cried and she no longer came, I knew... I was a man. Si-ci-di! Yiz!

Lazarus dances the Boot Dance for himself

Darkness

CURTAIN

LES FEMMES NOIRES
(Black Women)

First production – April to December 1976. New York Public Festival Theatre, New York City. Directed by Novella Nelson. Produced by Joe Papp.

CAST

Mary Alice	Rosanna Carter
Carla	Norma Jean Darden
Carolyn	Rosemary Stewart
Rita	Anna Horsford
King Alfa	Bill Cobbs
Hounsi – also Cipo	Gylan Kane
Roberta	Lauri Carlos
Mother	Trizana Bevily

Original music by Wali Obara and Saint

London production (Winner of the Ethnic Arts Award) – 1981 Keskidee Theatre. European tour followed. Directed by Rufus Collins

Mary Alice	Janet Bartly
Carla	Cher Camerton
Carolyn	Dorett Thompson
King Alfa	T-Bone Wilson
Hounsi/Cipo	Trevor Ward
Prophet	David Haynes
Pee Wee	Witty Forde
Roberta	Pam Obermeyer

CHARACTERS

King Alfa	A cripple and a spirit
Hounsi (also Cipo)	The legs of King Alfa; an artist
Mary Alice	About forty, has difficulty walking
Carla	Sister of Mary Alice (younger)
Laverne-Verna	A woman
Rita	A neighbour of Mary Alice
Carolyn	Her niece
Carolyn's mother	
Roberta	A prostitute and neighbour
Hamm	A butcher, Rita's husband
Jackie	Prostitute friend of Roberta's
Erlene and Didi, Jackie	Three women
Cop	
Pee Wee, Prophet (blind) and Naphatali	Three Men

SET:
Let there be many televisions used throughout the play as transition points. The television is a constant object throughout the homes of Les Femmes Noires. The television and all the sadness contained there.

Author's Note

The articles are: Evening, about six, the time of transformation to the uncertainty of night. Those black women who are workers have been released to buses and trains. The action of the play should be polyscenic (occurring all around the audience).

The play was written from the viewpoint of a blind man perceiving sound.

SCENE I – Morning and the Workers

New York, morning. The city if you spread grey across the canvas: then the time is somewhere between October and November. With the coming of the cold, the faces seem uncertain. The bodies of the black women restructure the architecture of the city as they enter the buildings of the dead, wrapped in new colours they go out and all men hope

Enter King Alfa pulled on a cart by Hounsi. King Alfa could be somewhere in his forties. The black face is carved by the world. Let a beard hide the pain. Hounsi is younger, the face an African Dogan mask in which you see nothing except a mirror. The first sound heard is that of King Alfa. We are at Times Square and Forty-Second Street

KING ALFA   See the trouble with you, Hounsi, you don't know how to beg yet but you will.

HOUNSI   All this pussy out here, a nigger would have to be crazy to get married.

KING ALFA   See, it ain't just putting the hand out there. You got to learn how to take them backward and forward in time. Make them see the earth. Then make them glad they not you. That's when they give up the coins.

HOUNSI   Yes, King Alfa. *(Puts out cup and starts begging)* Could you spare a few coins?

People pass, observe and walk on without giving

KING ALFA   See what I mean? You don't know what you doing. You better give me back that cup. I can do bad by myself.

HOUNSI   You know something? This is one nasty ass city. You know that?

KING ALFA   Let me tell you it looks worse from down here. If you look at the city you die. You look at the people. That's what you look at.

Puts a few coins in the cup then gives it back to Hounsi

HOUNSI   Wasn't talking about no city. I was talking about the people. *(Spots someone)* Excuse me, could you help out my friend here? He doesn't have any legs. *(She drops her pocketbook and bends to pick it up)* Damn, Miss Telephone Lady. Excuse me miss, don't you work across the street at the Bell Telephone Office?

WOMAN   *(Very guardedly)* Why do you want to know?

HOUNSI   I see you, your desk is in the window.

WOMAN   Yes, it is. Be seeing you. *(Goes to leave)*

HOUNSI   There was another sister there a few months.

WOMAN   Yes, she had to leave. I just took the job last. *(Catches herself and wonders what she is doing standing there speaking to a stranger)*

HOUNSI   Yes, I used to see her all the time when I'd pass. But you know what? Them whities worked her to death. I noticed when she started she had the sweetest little ass and the next thing you knew she didn't have nothing no more. Be careful that they don't do that to you.

WOMAN   Thanks for the advice, but I really don't need it. *(Exits)*

HOUNSI   You will.

KING ALFA   You up there talking shit and ain't got a quarter. That's 'cause you a young man.

HOUNSI   Damn she got one of them high asses.

KING ALFA   She don't even see you, nigger. You don't look like nothing she's seen on TV, figure she must of had 'bout 20,000 hours by now in front of that set. So you ain't real to her.

HOUNSI   *(Spotting another passer, he bends gracefully and receives a quarter in his cup)* Thank you and may you have a day of sunlight.

The girl who drops the money in the cup walks a few steps and then pauses to say

GIRL   Damn, I didn't mean to give the nigger that much. *(Exits)*

HOUNSI   I'd like to stick my head about twelve feet up inside her –

KING ALFA   I don't know. Those young girls are lot of work, my man. You get you one of them ladies up there over thirty-five. All you got to do with them is give them that alcohol, pop them once and they out for the night. Anyway they the ones that got the bucks.

Young nurse passes

HOUNSI   What is it about nurses King Alfa, that makes me want to rape them?

KING ALFA   That's because they remind you of those church sisters.

HOUNSI   Hello!

High School girl passes. Her body is arrogance. She looks at King Alfa and then at Hounsi. She chews gum for a while and then with the detachment with which one might decide to let a roach live, she drops a dime into his cup and walks on.

High school girl, a poem for sunlight high school girl.

HOUNSI   Hi school girl
titties round and body new
let me look at (because I
need to) let me look at you.
It's the last time that I'll
see you before they use you to conquer me.
The last time that I'll see you
before they use you to conquer
me. And what will they become?
The ladies, the ladies? And what
will they become? Hi school girl.

Enter cop

COP   OK let's move it.

HOUNSI   Just spreading a little sunlight.

COP   Well, spread it somewhere else. This is my beat.

HOUNSI   Hey ain't you Eliot? Don't you remember me, Hounsi? We were in Junior High together remember? We used to get in trouble all the time.

COP   No, I ain't Eliot. You better move on here. *(To King Alfa)* You too, buddy.

HOUNSI   Your face got harder, but it's you. Come on Eliot. Don't you remember Hounsi?

COP   I told you that's not me. Now come on, let's go.

KING ALFA   We going. Come on Hounsi.

HOUNSI   *(Walking off)* Why is it that everybody I grew up with are either dead, turned into faggots or joined the Police Department?

KING ALFA   Why is the sky blue, nigger? Come on, let's go.

HOUNSI   *(Taking one last lingering look at the women)* And what will they become? The ladies, the ladies and what will they become...?

KING ALFA   *(Already pulling himself a good distance)* Nigger, will you come on?

Hounsi exits bowing, King Alfa before him on his cart

Darkness

SCENE II – Laverne in the Subway

The entrance is night. Waiting for train on platform. Laverne: warmness and over thirty, light-skinned, neat and elegant

They enter. Hounsi and Laverne. She is tastefully dressed. He looks poor. They look at prostrate body of a drunk and go around him to bench

LAVERNE   I'm cold, hold me.

HOUNSI   *(Putting arm around her)* Your body's hot.

LAVERNE   Is it? I think I'm catching a cold. Renee's got one.

HOUNSI   Hope you didn't give it to me.

LAVERNE   I hope you get it, nigger. *(Laughing, Hounsi looks to see if any police are around then lights cigarette.)*

See that you're going to start me off again. I did pretty good last week. I cut down to one pack a day.

HOUNSI   *(Laughing)* Oh yeah!

LAVERNE   You don't know how hard that is. You know what I have to go home to now? A daughter who hates me.

HOUNSI Renée?

LAVERNE She despises me. Everytime I look at her, I see my husband's face. She's his daughter really, not mine. *(After pause)* But she's like me in a lot of ways. *(Pause)* You know what it was like married to a white man for four years? *(She takes cigarette from him)* Give me a drag. He used to like to just exhibit me and sit around and suck the life out of me.

HOUNSI For four years?

LAVERNE For four years, that's how crazy I was. And now he wants to take her and have my spirit that way. You know what I mean? That was my function for him, to make him a black baby that might save him. Meanwhile, here's my family cheering me on. My mother thought it was just great that her daughter was – *(Brings herself to full stop)* But that's all right, I'll deal with it. He's not going to get her. What do you do when you find yourself thinking too much?

HOUNSI I start painting on some walls.

LAVERNE Any walls?

HOUNSI Any walls. Come on, train's coming.

She takes his hand. Bum wakes up for a second then falls back asleep

Darkness

SCENE III – Study for Numbers-Woman

Two women relatively same age, mid-forties; Mrs Fowler, the numbers-woman has a soft Southern face and eyes which make you feel safe. Mrs Thompson, the second lady has come to place a figure in. She gives Mrs Fowler her slip very gently as though placing money in a collection plate at church

MRS FOWLER   So, how you today, girl? *(Looking at slip)* Oh, you going try the 948 again? That's your old standby, uh?

MRS THOMPSON   That's my husband J.J.'s number. He gone now. Been dead 'bout eight years. Whenever I dream on J.J., I play 948.

MRS FOWLER   Well, it's about due.

MRS THOMPSON   You been away, uh?

MRS FOWLER   Heah girl, I went to Europe.

MRS THOMPSON   To Europe?

MRS FOWLER   Yeah, I went with Miss Simpson, you know she lives on Boston Road. We went with her church. I got to see the Pope.

MRS THOMPSON   No fooling?

MRS FOWLER   Yeah, child. *(Looking at slip)* You want to put that in combination or straight?

MRS THOMPSON   No, I'm going put that in straight.

MRS FOWLER   There was a lot of ministers and cardinals and whatnot there. There was even one little coloured one.

MRS THOMPSON   A cardinal?

MRS FOWLER   Yeah, honey, a cardinal. Of course, I didn't care for Italy that much though. People drive too fast there. They must not want to live too long. *(Back to slip)* How many days you want to leave this in for?

MRS THOMPSON   'Til Wednesday.

MRS FOWLER   But I like Paris. Pari as they say. 'Cause they keep the streets so clean there. And the food, girl. They must have some kind a soul from somewhere, 'cause them people can cook. You know my nephew, Roger, was there in the war?

MRS THOMPSON   Roger?

MRS FOWLER   You know the boy I raised. He went crazy in service. He in that Veterans' home.

MRS THOMPSON   Oh yeah, Roger, that was your nephew.

MRS FOWLER   Anyway, he always say, Annie, you'd like Paris. *(Pause)* Wasn't many coloured there except for the Algerians and they mostly clean the street. And the Frenchmen, girl let me tell you. They are something else again. You can't even sit down for the men there. They be on you. They love them some black women. As they say, Les Femmes Noires. That's all you could hear was Les Femmes Noires.

MRS THOMPSON   I ain't never been anywhere. I'd like to, but I'm scared to fly.

MRS FOWLER   Oh, it ain't nothing, you just drink one of them Martinis and you fall right to sleep. You don't feel nothing. *(Pause and looking again at slip)* Is this 333?

MRS THOMPSON   Let me see. Yes, that's 333.

MRS FOWLER   I thought so. But seems like you crossed it out. *(Looking through glasses which hang from her neck on chain)*

MRS THOMPSON Well, I got to go put my black coat in the cleaners. I got to go to a funeral. Mr Stevens dead.

MRS FOWLER No fooling?

MRS THOMPSON He's the fourth person I know of died this week.

MRS FOWLER Must be the winter.

MRS THOMPSON Must be. *(In a whisper)* You know, Mr Stevens didn't have no money to be buried. We had to take up a collection in the building. His church going bury him. I would sure hate for something like that to happen to me. That's why I got my money down already for my tombstone.

MRS FOWLER Not me. I figure when you're dead, you're dead. It's over. It's somebody else's problem. I ain't worrying myself.

MRS THOMPSON I wouldn't be able to rest easy.

MRS FOWLER I'd rest just fine. You better find you some peace while you still can instead of spending all your money on some damn tombstone.

MRS THOMPSON Well, I got to go.

MRS FOWLER Okay, so you want this 'til Wednesday? All right dear. Take care yourself.

MRS THOMPSON Be seeing you. *(Turns to go and then stops to ask)* Hey, what was it they called you all over in Paris?

MRS FOWLER They called us Les Femmes Noires.

Mrs Thompson exits laughing. Mrs Fowler returns to her policy slip

Darkness

SCENE IV – The Father and the Son

King Alfa and Hounsi. The house of King Alfa is filled with stacks of newspapers

HOUNSI   *(As if continuing conversation about the girl in preceding scene)* What was that about?

KING ALFA   That was here before you. It's going to be here after you.

HOUNSI   People get kind of lost out here, King Alfa.

KING ALFA   Lost for days. But I got the whole thing catalogued. I got charts of it all.

HOUNSI   You sure got a lot of newspapers.

KING ALFA   I got files that go back thirty years. I'm going bring these motherfuckers up on charges. Crimes against humanity. And I'm going to be the judge.

HOUNSI   I hear you.

KING ALFA   *(Pulls himself along to stage right)* In this box over here I got my files on the Black Bourgeoisie. Studies on Virginia, mostly, and Atlanta. You got a lot of that Black slave owner money down there. Over here, I've got my files on the Jews. How much property they own up here in Harlem? *(Pulls himself along a little further)* Over here, I have my files on the history of the Trade Unions, and them civil service, got me 'bout three boxes on them.

HOUNSI   We some well informed slaves. *(Laughing)*

KING ALFA   We *the* most informed slaves this world ever known. But we see. Monk say, we see.

Lighting turns to green

KING ALFA Come here boy, I want to show you something. *(Hounsi bends down as if to receive some secret word)* You know how to deal with these? *(Takes out dice)*

HOUNSI Not too good.

KING ALFA See with dice it's not what you roll, but how. It's got to be continuous. *(Rolling dice smoothly)* This is the ritual of the world here. See these little dots, these are people falling out into the streets.

HOUNSI People?

KING ALFA People falling out into a street. And it's not what you shooting, it's the rhythm. Here, you try it.

HOUNSI *(Shooting dice)* Like that?

KING ALFA No, keep your hands closed until the throw is over. *(His face begins to take on the appearance of black leather)* Just like people in a street. Bush people who stay in hiding *(Throwing dice as he speaks)* Everybody's cool as long as they don't try to take over each other's space. You see when somebody gets in the way of a throw, they interfere with the rhythm. Then they got to die. Never take too much. Just what you need. Always leave a little bit for the ancestors. Don't be greedy, that's what happened to whitie, he got a greed jones, that's why he's dying. Don't mess with the rhythm and everything be right on time. Here take them. *(King Alfa hands dice to Hounsi. Hounsi shoots)*

Darkness

SCENE V – Study for Underworld

Visible is a large booth with a small money window as in a subway booth. The sound of a small transistor radio is heard at first and then a conversation between two Black voices

Two Black women, one older, one younger

VOICE I   Did you hear about that woman on 116th Street last night?

VOICE II   No, what happened?

VOICE I   She got her throat cut right in the subway.

VOICE II   These people crazy. I don't never take the subway home late at night.

Enter Cop from upstairs

COP   Hey, Carol, in there?

VOICE I   She don't come on until six today, Eliot.

COP   How you doing, Vickie?

VOICE I   All right. Is it raining up there?

COP   No, not yet. Looks like it's going to though. See you.

Cop exits

VOICE I   See you. Can't tell nothing down here.

VOICE II   It's getting cold that's all I know. Cover up that hole there's a draught coming in here.

VOICE I   Either there ain't no air at all or it's blowing you away down there.

Woman comes to window

WOMAN   Two, please.

Tokens are given and cover is replaced at window

VOICE II   What you do over the weekend?

VOICE I   Nothing. I went to the movies Saturday. Sunday I went up to see my brother at Danamora.

VOICE II   Your brother's at Danamora?

VOICE I   He sure is there. He goin' be there a while too. Arm Robbery. Fool!

VOICE II   Cedar works there.

VOICE I   Oh yeah. I didn't know that. Tommy say he didn't do it, but he lies so damn much. I don't know.

VOICE II   Cedar don't like working there.

Man comes to booth

MAN   One. Hurry up my train's coming.

He goes running for train soon as he gets token

VOICE II   Niggers are always rushing you. He ain't going no place. Running to go nowhere.

VOICE I   I know it.

A man comes running on and goes through without paying.

VOICE II   Did you see him? Hey, you can't go through there, you got to pay. Call the transit cop, Vickie.

VOICE I   What for? It don't make no difference. They ain't going raise your salary none.

VOICE II   I hate to see people getting away while everybody else got to pay.

VOICE I   This don't have nothing to do with me. I just work here. I ain't going to be here too long no way. I don't like being under no ground like some damn mole or something. Too many rats down here for me.

VOICE II   Where that cop at. It's going to be rush hour in a minute. Hand me that cheeseburger in that bag.

People start piling in. Use of Full Cast

Oh Lord, here they come.

They dissolve into a crowd of workers being released at five o'clock. They enter the catacombs mostly in twos, mainly women. Usually the pairs are made up of one attractive and one oversized. Some of the women carry umbrellas. They differ from the crowd at morning in that they look less optimistic and less groomed. They usually hold their umbrellas upside down now as if they didn't know what to do with them

The saxophone may be used here to simulate a train

This motion climaxes with the arrival home at various locations on the stage where different televisions are situated

Dissolve to darkness

SCENE VI – Evening and the Workers

Music: Coltrane & Ellington: Stevie

Entrance: Stage filled with blackness of bodies. Workers returning home: blind man Junkie (The Prophet), Roberta, Hamm, etc. Enter behind Mary Alice. She is about forty. She has a slight palsy of the legs. Her affliction does not stop her life force. Her hands are very soft especially in the centre. She walks with her cane. The setting is her apartment in a project.

MARY ALICE   *(After fixing drink and sitting wiggling her toes)* Thank you Jesus!

Enter Carla

CARLA   *(Talking to herself)* Damn, they sure worked my ass today. What's on that television?

MARY ALICE   Nothing. *(Continues to mutter to herself as she adjusts the dials)*

CARLA   John Lyons is crazy, standing over me like a hawk all day. *(Pause)* How you doing?

MARY ALICE   Can't complain. I had a hard time getting home on the subway. It seems like everyday those kids get larger. They'll knock you down and won't even know what –

CARLA   *(Cutting Mary Alice off)* I ran into that guy from 12B in the hallway. *(Thinking to herself)* He would have to see me after a day in the mines.

MARY ALICE   *(Continuing with her conversation)* And not a one of them kids would give me a seat. They're as bad as their parents.

CARLA   I wonder what he does? *(To herself)* Probably got a job with Model Cities or something. He looks like that type.

MARY ALICE   You didn't hear a word I said. You up there worrying about 12B. *(Pause)* They didn't make these streets in New York for me. Matter of fact they weren't thinking about me at all when they built this place. It's going to be winter soon and the hawks going to be out there. I know I'm not going to be able to walk in that snow. Sure would like to get to Jamaica for a week or so.

CARLA   *(Laughs)* Jamaica, me, too. I'm hungry.

MARY ALICE   Fix yourself something.

CARLA   I'm not that hungry.

MARY ALICE   You one lazy girl.

CARLA   Girl, let me tell you what happened to me at lunch. After that John Ass Lyon ran his mouth all morning. We had this short meeting with the Inner City Consortium. Talk about a slave ship full of niggers.

MARY ALICE   Uhm um Uhm um.

CARLA   Anyway, I told Gloria let's go get a drink. She was ready too. So we went to that bar Smithy's sister-in-law works at. You know the one. I must have had two Tom Collins – *(Thinking to herself sadly)* Well, it could have been four. Anyway, Gloria was practically falling off the stool. She said I must have been drunk the way I was shaking my ass on the way to the bathroom. Now, Mary you know I never shake my ass, do I?

MARY ALICE   No, Carla, you never shake your ass.

CARLA   I guess she said that 'cause that dried up ole nigger man grabbed my arm on the way. Talking about, 'Hey baby I didn't know you was working today. I got some money, you want some money?' Pulling out some dirty raggedy dollar bills saying, 'How much money you want? I gots lots of money.' I said, 'As long as you live, you ain't never going to have that much money.'

MARY ALICE   You sure can be cold, Carla.

CARLA   Yes, but he got the message that time. Bill call?

MARY ALICE   No, I just got in a few minutes before you.

CARLA   Oh, I guess I'll go take a bath then. Let me see. *(Pause, thinking to herself)* Who should I be tomorrow? *(Thinking to herself)* Goddess of the Nile? Maybe a black space voyager. Who should I be tomorrow, Mary?

MARY ALICE   Be yourself. *(Sits sipping her drink)*

CARLA   Yeah, but which one? *(Freeze frame)* You know something? I don't believe anybody really believes in this black thing. Do you think anybody takes it seriously? Everybody's just making money.

MARY ALICE   Must be somebody who believes in it.

CARLA   Put it this way, we the only people crazy enough to believe in something like freedom.

RITA   *(Her voice is coming from off-stage)* Hey, Mary, Carla, you all home? *(Knock is heard)* Hey, Mary!

MARY ALICE   Why don't you wear your blue what is it? That long blue dress.

CARLA   Oh, you mean the midi? Yeah, that would be all right, but I've kind of been going away from that image. *(She goes to open door. Mary is laughing at her last remark)* Mary, my new disguise... And how are you Mrs Howard?

MARY ALICE   *(To herself)* Carla's out of her damn mind.

Enter Rita, about thirty, still has youthful body which is miraculous after four children. Following behind Rita is Carolyn about age twenty-three, light-skinned, small innocent-sized breasts

RITA   What you all laughing about? I'm still living girl, this here is my cousin Carol – *(Turns and yells loudly to Mary)* This here is my cousin Carolyn.

MARY ALICE   Hi, how you doing? *(They walk in, the girl looks timidly at Mary and then smiles falsely)* Oh, she's a pretty little thing, did you just come to New York?

RITA   Yeah, she just got here. This boy she's going with left her in this hotel.

CAROLYN Please, don't do that. I never would have come to you if I knew you were going to –

RITA Why, it's the truth, ain't it? I ain't telling no lie, am I? Anyway he ran off with her money. Now she wants to get back to Cincinnati, and I ain't got no money to give her.

CAROLYN I can make it. *(Picks up Mary's cane and begins to toy with it)*

RITA You can make it my hiney!

CARLA She in college?

CAROLYN Yes. *(Pause)* Well, I was anyway.

RITA You'd better get your behind back there if you want to survive, 'cause you're too kind-hearted. You the kind of girl give a nigger everything she got then turn around and drink yourself sick, like Sylvia.

CAROLYN I ain't Sylvia.

MARY ALICE How much you need? I got ten if that'll help you.

RITA She need a hundred dollars.

MARY ALICE A hundred dollars! Well, like I said if ten will help you.

RITA I can't ask Hamm for no more. It's hard enough to get a nigger to marry you when you single, never mind with four like me. *(Turns to Carla)* Carla, do you think you –

CARLA No way! I'm already behind on next month's pay check, figure that one out. I'm still trying to catch up with what I owe.

Enter Roberta, knocking but not waiting for a response

ROBERTA   (*About thirty-five, a prostitute and too heavy to be comfortable*) Anybody see a man carrying a Hi-Fi set, a colour TV and a FM radio going down in the elevator?

CARLA   I didn't see no one.

RITA   What's the matter girl, they rob you again?

ROBERTA   Goddamit, it's the third time. Must be somebody that know when I'm out. Hell, I moved out of Harlem 'cause I was tired of being robbed. Now I'm spending three times as much rent, and I'm still being robbed.

RITA   I didn't see nothing, but I was up on your floor visiting Cathy, but I didn't see nobody different.

MARY ALICE   You call the police?

ROBERTA   What damn good are they? They can't find nothing to do with themselves except try to arrest me for what was it they called it? Morality or Morals. What was it that tired whitey said to me in court? Some old nonsense. You're an indecent person. They ain't got no time to be studying about my TV and Hi-Fi set.

RITA   Ain't it the truth.

ROBERTA   These police ain't nothing. Did I tell you I saw two of them shooting up? In uniform up in the Bronx. You think I'm lying?

RITA   In uniform and they was shooting up?

ROBERTA   If I'm lying, I'm flying. I saw these two dudes, I said, well they must be taking a smoke break. Then I dug them up close and realized that ain't no smoke break, they up there nodding.

RITA   Roberta, this is my cousin, Carolyn.

ROBERTA   How you doing girl?

CAROLYN   Fine.

ROBERTA   You sitting over there so quiet.

RITA   Her boyfriend, should I say ex-boyfriend.

CAROLYN   Oh, you just going to tell the world uh?

RITA   Ain't nobody here going to do you no harm.

MARY ALICE   Come here Carolyn. *(Takes her quietly off to the side)*

RITA   Anyway he ripped her off for about a hundred dollars, and we're trying to get it up for her so she can go back home.

ROBERTA   That's a nigger for you. Ran off with the money. Don't worry. If I can turn these two tricks tonight, I'll let you have some money.

CAROLYN   He couldn't help it, he was just trapped. This white man's capitalism is going to kill us all.

ROBERTA   She may be real smart, but she ain't too bright. What did she just say, did she say he couldn't help it?

RITA   That's what she said.

ROBERTA   Listen, my little bit of change is too hard to come by. I be working on my back. I got to go.

RITA   Don't pay this child no mind, Roberta. This here is Alice in Wonderland, but she's going to learn. If you get anything let me know 'cause she's family, right, hard head or not.

ROBERTA   What's your name, Carol?

CAROLYN   Carolyn. One thing I can't understand.

How come everybody just stands around on the streets here. Just looking like zombies?

RITA   They looking at each other that's all.

CAROLYN   All day long?

ROBERTA   So much going on all the time in them streets.

CAROLYN   But nothing's going on.

ROBERTA   Just depends on what you looking at. Us women got to take care of each other 'cause the niggers are out to lunch. Lord, the girl looks so sad. You going to be all right. I'll see you later, Rita.

She exits

RITA   I got some clothes I want you to try on. They can't fit me no more, I can't be running around looking fly anyway. I ought to kick your ass girl. You sure simple.

CAROLYN   Go home? Go home to what? It's like a tomb in my house.

RITA   You're safe there at least.

CAROLYN   There's got to be more to life than being safe.

RITA   That's because you don't have any babies, no responsibilities. You don't know how lucky you are. I was like you once, living in a dream. Just walking around asleep. But people can hurt you girl. They'll do it every time, you'll wake up and find yourself alone with three babies to take care of. You're young, you're in school, stay your ass there. Believe me there's a lot more women than there are men.

CAROLYN   I know it.

RITA   Well, you don't act like you know it. Don't let people take advantage of you. Love yourself more than that. I didn't you know, people told me I was attractive and I never believed it. I felt guilty because I was light-skinned.

CAROLYN   Oh, come on.

RITA   I really did. I always had the best. I was 'Miss Most Likely To Succeed' and I still felt guilty... Seems as if I went out and looked to get hurt and you're the same way.

CAROLYN   I don't know why you keep thinking you know me when you don't understand at all.

RITA   Mary you talk to her. I'm weak already. Let me get back to this apartment before those kids make a total wreck of it... I'll be next door.

CARLA   What's your sign Carolyn? *(Rita exits)*

CAROLYN   Cancer. Why?

CARLA   Nothing, just wondered... *(Carla exits)*

CAROLYN   *(Figures silently dissolve around her)* He said, 'Wait here for me 'cause I have to take care of some business.' I knew he was lying, 'cause his eyes was lying. It's like watching yourself being undressed. You know it's happening but you're letting it happen. You say please don't be like all the other men I know about, please don't be so obvious. And I'll be goddam if he didn't go on anyway. Sometimes you just get tired. *(She exits)*

MARY ALICE   *(Alone)* Carolyn, you have such a nice straight back. *(Tries to stand up tall like Carolyn)* This is the part of night I like best. Silence. So high up you don't hear the screams so much. So high up I didn't think a rat could reach up here, but it might. Early evening is prettier, after sunset. It's almost worth the rent here just to see that . But usually there is so much commotion here, you can't enjoy it. The time of day when the sky gets so dark and lumps of white cloud dissolve till you can't tell which is sky and which is cloud.

That gets me through the day while I'm in the office watching people kill each other quietly, and it's only because it's done so quiet that you realize you're not in the gutters. Everyday the desk that you work at gets older, and the longer you work at one place the better risk you are. So now you can get a loan which keeps you working there a little longer.

Every year somebody dies, they take up contributions, or they buy you a watch when you retire.

Sometimes when I'm coming home on the trains, I look to see if the conductor is a brother. I feel safer when it's a brother driving. I know he won't kill me because he don't want to die himself. When the train comes from underground at a Hundred-and-Twenty-Fifth Street, everybody is so shocked to see sunlight. They're not creatures for a minute, they have eyes like children and they stop breathing like beasts for a minute. When I dream I can always walk perfectly. I'm like a dancer then. My back is just as straight as Carolyn's. The muscles on my thighs love each other and knit themselves together just right.

Everything is so smooth in dreams, streets are marble like glass. No concrete anywhere to trip over, and the sunlight or the night stars always hit the walls of the temples just right. Just enough to make them jewels. *(Takes up glass again)* When I drink, it relaxes me. The nerve ends go to sleep, and my breathing slows down. *(Sits down flexing and unflexing her legs)*

Can't complain though, can't complain. I could be twenty and have niggers scheming how to use me, or I might have to live my life all over again days and nights. Like when my father said, 'Girl, you black, you poor, and cripple. You can't even play no piano, you're just the last inkspot.' He thought that was funny.

People just open their mouths and words come all out. You know, I'm beginning to think if nobody is watching, then no one is really kind.

Pause

You know.

SCENE VII – Reunion: (Carolyn's Space)

Carolyn seated in a peculiar darkness. Stage should be lighted from below if possible in this scene

CAROLYN   And I'll walk into the house. And the living room will smell like it was just dusted. And I'll move from inside my mother's arms and into my father's. And then they'll look at me close to see if I'm pregnant.

Mama, why you looking at me like that? As if you're looking for something wrong with me? What did I do in the city? I was a waitress for a while, I'd wear white tights and this little black shirt and an apron. I'd serve all these strange people and try not to look in their faces.

Am I going to go back to school? Yeah, mama, I'm going to go back. Eventually. But listen, mama, I want to tell you about the streets I saw there. And those faces mama. Black faces. So many tribes. Eyes crazy. Can't tell the people from the garbage, mama. And these old ladies carrying shopping bags and sleeping in the train stations. And the junkies bend like trees. Except there are no trees 'cause it's New York, mama.

Cipo, artist and crazy, also Carolyn's lover, enters

CIPO   Morning, touch of sunlight to a running sky
Little black waitress
small little titties laying up
head moving like a lady.

CAROLYN   *(Turning around)* What are you doing here? This is my father's house. You can't be here.

CIPO   Can't be anywhere so I might as well be here.

CAROLYN   Cipo why you lie so much? Why you got to lie to me? You had me –

CIPO   Remember that one-legged man asleep leaning on that parking meter?

CAROLYN   I remember.

CIPO   And those grey tenement houses, sometimes sunlight trying to leak between them?

CAROLYN   And the hallways narrow that you said were death?
And the backyards and the gates on the windows that
you said was death? But as long as you were there with me
everything was all right. As long as you were there. You know.

CIPO   Long as, brother-man
            Long as brother man
            You can be, let me take you by the hand.
            You can be, you can be a pussy or an owl.
            A pussy or an owl.
            They hurt the pussy, baby
            Everyday they going to hurt him
            but dig the owl, dig the owl
            up in the tree, laying up between the
            darkness and leaves.
            He just be hooting, HOOT.
            see, like this HOOT! That's all the
            Motherfucker says. Who was it that told me
            that?

   Tries to recall

CAROLYN   Hey, come back please.

CIPO   Sorry, I hear these voices. Hounds out of hell. My mind gets flooded with voices and faces, too many faces.

CAROLYN   And that's when you start running to dope.

CIPO   It's going to be all right though. Everything going to be cool after a while.

CAROLYN   'Cause why?

CIPO   'Cause you move like a lady.

CAROLYN   I can't do for you. I was there totally, body all open. And you ran.

CIPO   Everything going to –

CAROLYN   Going to be what?

CIPO   Clear light, light of the sun. Hey listen. *(Whispers something to her. She refuses him, he takes her hand gently rubbing it along his fly)* Hey, listen.

CAROLYN   No, that's not going to get it. You had your chance.

CIPO   Come on Carolyn, right now.

CAROLYN   Not in my father's house.

CIPO   I remember your father. He put his face in the doorway and his eyes said, 'I know you boy and I really don't like you.'

CAROLYN   He said you were very talented.

CIPO   The middle class always like talent if they can figure out a way to make some money off it. If they can't make no money from you, then they try to put your ass in prison or some insane asylum.

CAROLYN   That's not what bothers you. It's the fact that people don't even see you that drives you crazy.

CIPO   It's a weird time. I'm thirty years old, and nobody ever heard of me.

CAROLYN   You as scared as I am.

CIPO   I'm tired of circles baby, I know I've been in this world before. It's bad enough living it once but I'm a son of the fifth generation and like I was walking through the streets of Rome and I'm digging all the flames and nobody else seems to notice. You understand?

CAROLYN   You've been living in that goddam city too long.

CIPO   I am the city.

CAROLYN   Concrete and old women stealing from

garbage cans. You got that! I need a little rest for a while.

CIPO You think this is going to be a rest. Okay. Catch you a little later on. Next time you want to play some more games with poverty, because you're Morning touch of sunlight to a running sky.

Exits

CAROLYN I can't deal with you. You crazy. They told me about you. You're not safe. Let me turn here to some hands which I know. Hello, Mama.

MOTHER *(Late forties, restrained in her wig, a lot of tension in her eyes)* I'm glad you came home.

CAROLYN Yes, Mama.

MOTHER You look a little thin. You lost weight. *(As if touching Carolyn's face, the actress is facing audience)*

CAROLYN No, don't.

MOTHER I just want to touch you.

CAROLYN No, Mama. I'm not pregnant.

MOTHER I didn't ask you that.

CAROLYN I had my period last week just like I was supposed to. Hurt like hell too.

MOTHER You haven't seen the house since I changed it around. Do you like it?

CAROLYN It looks like you.

MOTHER Your father's been worried about termites.

CAROLYN He ran off and left me, Mama.

MOTHER Well, I'm glad that's over. You'll feel better soon.

CAROLYN   No, I won't.

MOTHER   Celia's been asking about you. She's getting married next month.

CAROLYN   That's nice.

MOTHER   To Paul Vincent. He's head of that black law firm now and Cindy's about to graduate.

CAROLYN   You never told me about New York, Mama.

MOTHER   Told you what?

CAROLYN   You never told me about how women's bodies can look like men. Tired like men.

MOTHER   I couldn't tell you.

CAROLYN   You never told me the way a man goes crazy when he doesn't have any money.

MOTHER   A man could get a job if he was a man.

CAROLYN   You never told me about niggers.

MOTHER   Be glad for that. Be careful for the rug, dear, with those cigarette ashes.

CAROLYN   *(More to herself)* Why do you do that?

MOTHER   Are you all right sweetheart? It's winter. I remember how you hate winter. You don't like it when the sun goes away.

CAROLYN   I'm fine.

MOTHER   You know how you get into those moods. You lock yourself all up in your room. You don't talk to anyone. You're sure you're all right? If you want to see that doctor again –

CAROLYN   No, I'm not crazy anymore.

MOTHER   Oh, we know you're not.

CAROLYN   Insanity is a luxury of the middle class.

MOTHER   *(Laughing)* What? Where did you get that one from?

CAROLYN   I think I'm going to go upstairs for a little while Mama.

Carolyn exits

MOTHER   All right dear, your father is going to be home at six. We're so glad you're home, Carolyn. Tomorrow we'll go shopping downtown. Get you a few new dresses and some shoes. You'll feel so much better, you'll see. We'll take the car, and you can drive it, if you want to, just the way we used to. With your face which is my face younger. And when they see us together, when the others see us, they'll stop and say, there goes Mrs Johnson and her daughter Carolyn. She's home now.

Darkness

SCENE VIII - Meanwhile in Golgotha

Pee Wee about forty and from the South is standing talking drunk, loud, and lonely. Roberta enters. Dinah Washington's 'What a Difference a Day Makes' and Aretha's 'I Ain't Never Loved A Man The Way That I Love You'

The name Golgotha's is hanging over bar

Verna, age difficult to determine. Very man-like with her movements

VERNA   So this girl on my job, Yvonne, you know. She a fool anyway. She been working there for ten years in that hospital. Like I told her, I ain't hardly going to be working in no one job for no ten years. Hell they lucky if I finish out this one.

Anyhow she come into work today looking all pitiful and what not, her eyes all messed up. I say what happened girl? She say her husband and her got into a thing and he hit her. I said what you going do? She said 'I ain't going get him mad no more.'

I said, hell, if that would of been me, his behind would have been in that court room, you can believe that. And when I go in there, I'd sure would be looking bad. I'd have more bandages on my face then a little bit. Have me some doctor's certificate sign sealed and delivered. When come time for me to testify, I'd testify for days. I'd talk about the sucker so bad his mama wouldn't want him no more. I'd put that shit right out there. When I got through they'd put his ass under the jail. You think I'm lying?

PROPHET You something else Verna.

VERNA What, some nigger going to hit me? Hell, if I took him to court he should get on his knees and thank me that I didn't throw some boiling water in his motherfucking face. He getting off easy if I take him to court.

PROPHET Girl, you cold.

VERNA No, listen, I am my mother's daughter, Miss Bessie Lou Philips Stevens, and don't no nigger raise his hand to me. I done seen too much of that shit. We buddy buddy and everything's cool, just don't raise your hand to me.

PROPHET Amen, sister.

VERNA   Amen my ass.

Enter Pee Wee returning from bar

PEE WEE   That woman got to be crazy think I'm going to kill my damn self for her. I'll be in my grave and she'll be running around here talking about how she loved me. Don't make no sense, right?

PROPHET   Right, Pee Wee.

PEE WEE   Hey Roberta, come here honey, you not going to say hello to me?

ROBERTA   How you doing, Pee Wee? You loaded again?

PEE WEE   What if I am? You bad as my wife. I can't have no fun, right.

ROBERTA   You can do any damn thing you want to.

Looking around for somebody

PEE WEE   My Papa used to say it's a free country long as you got the money.

ROBERTA   Thought you told me you never knew your papa.

PEE WEE   This guy wasn't my father, I just called him Papa. Let me buy you a drink.

ROBERTA   I'm trying to find somebody.

PEE WEE   *(He drops down in a chair and starts counting a fistful of dollars)* You ain't going let me buy you a drink?

ROBERTA   Yeah, OK. *(Eyeing money)* I'll have a rum and coke.

PEE WEE   All right. Rum and coke for the lady. Think I'm just going lay with my Gordon Gin. *(As he gets up from table and goes to bar she turns and calls to someone)*

ROBERTA   Hey, Jackie, you see Sharkey in here tonight?

JACKIE   *(Walking over to the table, she could be in late twenties, early thirties. She has a razor cut across face)* He ain't been through here all night. Somebody else been looking for him.

ROBERTA   Damn girl, what happen to your face?

JACKIE   That crazy old bitch Rochelle. We were just sitting around Monday evening over at Fat Mack's getting high. Her and Gladys got into this argument. I wasn't paying them no mind, I was just sitting there enjoying my high, next thing I knew this girl had her razor out. I couldn't believe it.

ROBERTA   But why she cut you?

JACKIE   You know that girl out her damn mind anyway. She was in one of them institutions. I don't know why they let her ass out. She thought I was laughing at her. I was going to kill her, I swear to God. Mack separated us. Like he said, he really didn't know what she was doing 'cause she's crazy.

ROBERTA   She'd have to be more than crazy to get away with cutting my face up.

JACKIE   And you know I could feel that something was going to happen to me Monday. I could just tell that something was going to touch me close.

PEE WEE   *(Re-entering with drink)* Here you go, Miss Roberta. *(Looking at Jackie's face)* Damn girl, what happened to you?

ROBERTA   She got cut.

JACKIE   What's it look like happen to me?

PEE WEE   Looks like you was in the wrong place at the wrong time.

JACKIE   Well, that's what happened.

ROBERTA   Why don't you buy Jackie a drink and cheer her up?

PEE WEE   What the matter, you feel bad about that little scar? You still a fox.

> *Enter Naphtali carrying two shopping bags. He wears sneakers and dungarees. He is a shoplifter. A very good shoplifter*

NAPHTALI   What happening people? Anybody want some clocks?

JACKIE   I don't need no clocks.

ROBERTA   Me neither, you got any radios or televisions?

NAPHTALI   No, not today. I had some nice dresses about your size *(Looking at Jackie)* this afternoon, but I didn't see you around.

JACKIE   Oh, yeah?

NAPHTALI   *(Back to Roberta)* I'm going to be into some radios tomorrow. I'll stop by tomorrow night around midnight.

ROBERTA   Round about midnight? OK.

PEE WEE   What you want to drink, little bit?

> *Jackie doesn't hear him, her mind is lost in the universe of the bar*

ROBERTA   Hey Jackie!

JACKIE   Huh?

NAPHTALI   Anybody interested in some silver crosses? You all might want to keep Dracula away *(Holds out a fistful of silver crosses)*

JACKIE   Vermouth.

PEE WEE   Vermouth?

ROBERTA   It's going to take more than a cross to keep Dracula away.

JACKIE   On second thought, a Rum and Coke.

NAPHTALI   *(To Pee Wee)* Hey man, this shirt should be about your size.

PEE WEE   Let me see.

NAPHTALI   Here goes another one. Let you have both of them for five dollars, they sell for ten apiece. Square business.

PEE WEE   I don't know man, I don't really need no shirts.

NAPHTALI   You always going need shirts my man. *(Leaves them with Pee Wee to consider, goes over to blind prophet)* Hey, Prophet, what's happening, where is it at?

PROPHET   Everybody's waiting on Sharkey.

NAPHTALI   Damn ain't nobody got nothing?

PROPHET   Not unless you want some methodone.

NAPHTALI   Hell, no!

PEE WEE   *(To Roberta)* How these shirts look to you?

ROBERTA   They pretty hip.

PEE WEE   Yeah okay, I'll take them Naphtali. Let me get this girl her drink. *(Naphtali follows Pee Wee off)*

ROBERTA   Whatever happened to those two dudes you picked up last Saturday?

JACKIE   Which two?

ROBERTA   Remember you was trying to get me to come along with you because you said they had money.

JACKIE   Oh yeah, they was freaks, honey. We went home with them, me and Lisa. They had a jar full of coke plus they were giving us fifty dollars apiece. So we snorting all this coke and then the oldest one takes out this movie projector, so I said let me see where this fool is coming from. You know he put on a stag film.

ROBERTA   A stag film?

JACKIE   Can you dig that, they got me and Lisa up there and they going to put on a film.

ROBERTA   That's what they needed to get they thing up?

JACKIE   *(Her mind wanders for a while and then)* Yeah.

PEE WEE   *(Returning with drink)* Here you go, Jackie.

JACKIE   Oh, that's for me. Thank you.

PEE WEE   Niggers is something else, boy. They stuck up my cab Wednesday night, two young cats. Put a razor right up to my throat. Shit, I wasn't going to argue with them. You can have the damn money. Just don't kill me. Wasn't but twenty-five dollars.

ROBERTA   I'd let them have the money every time. I just don't want nobody shooting or cutting on me.

PEE WEE   Now see my wife is the most greediest person living on this earth. She loves her money, man. She want to know why I didn't get my gun and chase them. I said, 'Shit, you must be crazy woman. If I don't never see them two again in life it's too soon for me.' She's Annie Oakley.

Aside to himself

You don't know how glad I am to get away from her. Go out and get me a little piece of pussy. Get a little drunk. Rest my mind for a minute. Hell, I deserve it.

JACKIE   Must have been because I didn't carry my little ball of cotton with me Monday. Always carry this piece of cotton for luck. Reminds me of when I was sixteen, we use to pick cotton when I'd go to Georgia, and it was good because we didn't have to pick it. We just did it 'cause we wanted to. It was white and soft and we could fall down and make love in the fields. *(Pause)* Come all the way up North to get my face scarred.

PEE WEE   You know, in all my life I ain't never met a woman really liked herself. Not one. Why you think that is? *(Both women hear him and decide to act as if they didn't)* Seem like no woman don't like herself.

ROBERTA   Wonder when Sharkey's going to get here?

JACKIE   I don't know, he should be passing through here sometime soon.

NAPHTALI   Silver crosses, people.

> Dinah Washington's, 'There is No Greater Love', background frozen
>
> Bar room scene people in a state of waiting at Golgotha's
>
> Dissolve to darkness

SCENE IX – Study for Two Ladies in Love

Background: Otis Redding's 'Your Precious Love'

Erlene and Didi. Erlene is the older, body androgynous, the way women's bodies become either from alcohol, dope, or life. Didi early twenties, thin, mischievous body. A predatory city night sky outlining them

ERLENE So what was he saying to you?

DIDI He wasn't saying nothing.

ERLENE I saw him laughing.

DIDI The usual. He was just running his thing, that's all. He wanted me to go with him. I told him that whichever way he was going I didn't want to go that way.

ERLENE Come grinning in my face. That nigger better look out.

DIDI Oh, he don't mean nothing. He was just gaming.

ERLENE I told that nigger before he better leave you 'lone.

DIDI It's getting cold out here.

ERLENE You should have worn your leather coat. You out here trying to be fly. You going catch pneumonia, you go on.

DIDI My titties hurting me. *(Hugs herself)*

ERLENE You something else, girl. Did you go to the doctor's to see about that swelling?

DIDI I can't go to no doctor, you know I'm scared of them. I can't stand nobody cutting on me.

ERLENE So what you going to do, fool? Just sit there and let it get worse? You such a little coward.

DIDI I know it.

ERLENE Look, I'll go with you.

DIDI Would you?

ERLENE Yeah, sure. We could go tomorrow. *(Didi is frightened)* Look how big her eyes get. Stop worrying, probably be okay.

DIDI You think so?

ERLENE The longer you wait, the worse it is.

DIDI I'm hungry.

ERLENE You just eat a minute ago.

DIDI *(Looking childish)* I don't care, I'm still hungry.

ERLENE Let's go in here and buy some ribs.

DIDI All right.

ERLENE You know I'll take care of you right? *(Touching her)*

DIDI I know Erlene.

ERLENE And you don't need no man.

DIDI If you say so.

They exit together

Darkness

SCENE X - Hamm The Butcher

As he is speaking in the background Mary Alice has a dream in which Carla, Carolyn, Rita and Roberta place old watches on her body. Hamm is busy at butcher's block

HAMM   So I married her. She had three of them little crumb snatchers and I married her anyway. Always loved me a woman with big titties. People tell me I'm crazy to marry any woman already got three children. Then here I come give her another one. But I figure like this, I ain't never going have no money no way. Not the way they got this country set up. If they even see me starting to make some money they going find some way to stop me. So I just say later for it. And went on and married her.

Pause

She all right. Crazy. But she cool. Got a lot of life. You need that, Jim. When I was nineteen and crazy, walking around didn't know nothing. Waiting on the light. Then I woke up and found my behind in the service.

Didn't never think of how it was a set up from the jump. Everybody I ever knew in my life had just set me up to land right there, a soldier boy. Every day I'm watching cats dying, place full of death. I said so this is what it's really all about eh? OK so what else can you show me? I said, no way. God can't be taking care of no kind of business, not with all these people dying. They let me entertain the troops with the USO because I could sing. I had a voice. I was in the Gospel Choir and what not. When I was young. So I got to travel with the Red Cross. So like, I got over. But I said damn, what if a nigger can't sing or play no instrument. He's going to be dead.

I be thinking about things like that. Life ain't no big thing. I guess I married Rita because between her and them little cannibals she got, I don't have no time to think about nothing. That's fine with me. All life is just a lesson, but it's a hell of a lesson.

Sometimes I catch Rita just staring off into space. The world be going through her mind. She sad for a little while but she gets it together. You better off having more than one kid in case one of them got to be sacrificed. At least that way you got something left. I don't know.

Ain't nothing happening

Pause

really.

Continues chopping meat

Darkness

SCENE XI - Epilogue

Mary Alice's apartment bedroom. The coming of night

CARLA   You know I was over Larry's last night.

MARY ALICE   Uh humm.

CARLA   And listen I was ready. He had some of that Johnny Walker Red.

MARY ALICE   I know you was.

CARLA   I was ready. Don't you know that little girl of

his, Loretta, started to perform and would not stop, honey?

MARY ALICE   How old is she?

CARLA   She ain't but three. But she had me know there wasn't going to be but one queen in that house. She wouldn't fall asleep.

MARY ALICE   So what you do?

CARLA   I couldn't do nothing. I came on home. I can't get into it with no child screaming in the next room.

MARY ALICE   Listen girl, if you would have really wanted to, you would have found a way.

CARLA   You know sometimes I get tired of myself.

MARY ALICE   What's on the television?

CARLA   Nothing. Sometimes I get real tired of myself. You think it could be I know myself too well?

MARY ALICE   I don't think that's it. I'm trying to reconstruct my life too. Maybe if I work harder.

CARLA   I don't think I'm ever going to be famous.

MARY ALICE   *(Laughing)* Ain't none of us going to be famous.

CARLA   When I was in High School, I was very bright, you remember that?

MARY ALICE   Yeah, you got the best grades.

CARLA   Seems like I started slipping when I left school. Started going to sleep. I just don't want to end up like them ladies in bars on Saturday listening to Aretha, talking loud, and lonely.

MARY ALICE   Don't worry, that's not going to be you.

CARLA   Mary Alice, I been thinking about getting a place of my own just so I could have a little freedom.

MARY ALICE   *(Turning and looking at her)* You been thinking about it? Why didn't you say something?

CARLA   I know how hard it is for you.

MARY ALICE   No, listen girl, please don't ever hold up your life for me. I think that's a wonderful idea. *(Aside)* Girl you don't know how happy I'd be.

CARLA   *(Laying down again)* It wouldn't be immediately.

MARY ALICE   Oh.

CARLA   If I'm asleep tomorrow morning wake me up when you get up.

MARY ALICE   *(Laying down)* You want me to wake you?

CARLA   Please, 'cause I know I'm going to be dead.

MARY ALICE   All right.

CARLA   This preacher suppose to be healing people at the grotto.

MARY ALICE   What preacher?

CARLA   The preacher, Amet. I was listening to him on the radio. People really be going for it.

MARY ALICE   He suppose to be able to heal people?

CARLA   That's what they say. He can put his hands

over your body and you don't feel no pain anymore, or something. He got a lot of followers. I can't sleep. I keep dreaming about this room full of crushed glass.

MARY ALICE   Where is this grotto at?

CARLA   On Rood Street, why?

MARY ALICE   I'm going to check him out.

CARLA   Do you believe that he - ?

MARY ALICE   No harm in trying is there?

CARLA   He's just telling people what they want to hear.

MARY ALICE   Then let him tell me what I want to hear. You just have to take it one day at a time, that's all.

CARLA   Well, it's up to you. *(Lays down)*

MARY ALICE   Think I'll wear my bright dress and walk on down to the grotto. *(Pause)* Here it comes now, watch the darkness. Lay down, clear lights, all peace.

Darkness

Curtain